ONE LITTLE SPECK

Gaynor Goodchild

pPp
PALACE PARK
PRESS

A catalogue record for this book is available from
the British Library.

ISBN 978-1-908318-47-3

Printed and bound by CPI Group (UK) Ltd, Croydon, CR0 4YY

PPP
PALACE PARK
PRESS

About the Author

Gaynor was born into a destructive alcoholic family and did her best to keep things together as a child. She soon found the burden too much and craved escape; unfortunately alcohol offered her that release.

She morphed from a quiet child at the back of the class to an abused addict whose daily life involved horrors most people couldn't imagine. Gaynor became trapped in violent, destructive cycles that left her isolated and destroyed.

However, she was determined to beat her demons for her own sake and for her daughter. She managed to turn her life around. She is now a qualified counsellor who hopes to help others with their addictions in the future. She lives in Essex and is a proud mum to her law-graduate daughter.

INTRODUCTION

Before making a start on my autobiography, I spent a considerable amount of time soul-searching; trying to understand why my desire to write was so strong. It was a feeling that didn't seem to desert me, returning time and time again, nagging away at the pit of my stomach, swirling around like a boat caught up in a storm, not going anywhere fast, but desperate to arrive to its destination.

I also asked myself am I writing this because I want to be famous?, which obviously I am not. Is it that I want to be recognised, to make money and be rich? The answer to all these questions is simply 'no'.

It's simple really, this 'little speck' which, when I realised how huge and crowded the universe is, is really all that I am in the greater scheme of things. I may be a 'little speck', but for someone so minute, there is a hell of a lot to me, Gaynor Goodchild.

I hope you enjoy the journey with me, with my traits, trials and tribulations that have made me into the person I am today.

CHAPTER ONE

MY ARRIVAL

I was born on the fourth of April 1963 at Perivale Hospital, Middlesex. I was not alone in the amniotic sac for nine months; I had some company there, my twin sister Pru. I must have tormented her to bits, for she escaped out of our mother's womb ten minutes before I had the chance to poke my head out and take a look around. It must have been confusing for me from the moment I found myself sliding out of the environment I had been surrounded in for so long. I was yanked out by my ankles, which must have felt rather strange, for my head was still saying goodbye to my abode which I must have sensed I would not be returning to again. Yes you got it, I was what they call a breach baby and Mum always said I went back for my comb. She also informed me later on in my life, that after giving birth to my twin, she forgot that I was still inside her and the midwife who delivered us, who Mum claimed was psychic, looked at me and told Mum, 'This one is going to push her way through life to get what she wants, no matter who gets hurt along the way.' *Charming!!!* Well, she certainly knew I was very much alive and kicking the minute I settled in to this new environment called life, here on earth, I made damn sure of that. No one was going to forget me in a hurry; I adopted this attitude from a very young and tender age.

As I grew a little, I discovered that it was not just my twin and I; there were three others in our family – two older brothers and one older sister. I can't remember much about my elder Sister, Diane, I did not know where she was; all I knew was that she was not living in the same house as the rest of us. I discovered later on that she had left England and was living in America. My brother Max, I can barely remember. My two strongest memories of him are when Mum went to the airing cupboard to get something and found his packet of condoms hidden in there. Mum wanted stern words, to say the least, but my brother scarpered out the back door. The other memory is of being woken up one night by what sounded like a war breaking out downstairs. When I tip-toed down the stairs like a little church mouse, I poked my head round the living room door and found my brother and father brawling on top of a tipped over settee. I did not stick around long enough to question this startling and rather disturbing occurrence, I went back up the stairs a hell of a lot quicker than I came down them.

I have many memories of my other brother, Pete, during this time –some very naughty ones I am afraid to say. He babysat for my sister and I when Mum and Dad went out in the evening, which was more often than not to the pub. On the way out, I would ask my dad 'where are you going Daddy?' He always replied 'To see a man about a dog.' I suppose at this tender age (I am not quite sure how old I was) I must have thought my mummy and daddy must love dogs very much, for they were always going out to see this man whoever he was, about these dogs, especially on Saturday nights. The only reason I knew it was a Saturday, was that on Saturday afternoons when I was in my room, (which later on in life became my little sanctuary) I would hear shouting and screaming. Mum and Dad always watched the horse racing and would beckon and encourage the horse that they had bet on to win. Later on the same day, I would see Mum looking in the mirror in the kitchen, applying her make-up and putting this ghastly smelly spray stuff all over her hair to keep it in place. I will never forget that awful smell, it seemed to fill the whole house and went right to the back of my throat, making me feel sick.

The second my parents left the house, the living room was transformed in the space of minutes. I was bewildered to see my brother Pete racing round the room like a mad bat out of hell, pumping all the pillows on the settee up, drawing the curtains, switching the little lamp on, which made the room look very cosy and warm. He had this strange looking object in his hands which was apparently a carpet sweeper (I'm not sure if Hoovers were invented then). He would push it backward and forwards like a man possessed. I had never seen the living room look tidy, apart from on Saturday nights.

My sister and I would be left with a bag full of sweets when they went out, but most of the time I only had the chance to taste a handful of them, for my brother Pete would play this so-called game with us. He would say to us 'Do you believe in fairies?'. With our little faces full of wonder, we replied 'don't know'. He then continued to say, 'If you close your eyes and hold out your hand with some sweets in, the fairies will come.' Excited, we stretched our little hands full of sweets. 'Don't open them until I tell you,' he said. Seconds later, he said 'Open your eyes now, the fairies have been'. With our eyes wide open, we looked down at our hands and our sweets had disappeared, when asked where our sweets had gone, he replied that the fairies had been and taken your sweets. I was so excited about the fairies, I forgot about the remaining sweets. It took me a long, long time until the penny finally dropped and I realised that it was not the fairies I was giving my sweets to, it was my brother and he was eating them all, the greedy little git.

His next move was to raid the kitchen, observing him he looked as though he hadn't eaten for years. He would gulp down scrambled eggs on toast. I doubt if he even tasted it by the speed the food got shovelled into his mouth. Next, we were carted off to bed, which seemed earlier than we usually went up the stairs. Mind you, normally there were no fixed bedtimes; you will discover why later on. What I did notice is that not long after my sister and I were tucked up in our beds, the front door would go, and being an inquisitive little madam right from the start of my life, I crept out of bed and stood a few steps down, just enough to see who was coming into the house. In walked a strange woman that I did not recognise, sometimes the same women would return time and time again on Saturday nights. I started to get a little concerned, for as the Saturday nights came round again, I would see many different-looking women coming through the front door. I worked out, as I grew a little more, that these women were my brother's girlfriends. Now things were starting to make sense, that's why my brother flew around the living room tidying up and setting a romantic scene with the dimmed lights and all, for he was preparing himself for a night of...! He basically had the house to himself. There was one particular woman that my brother had invited round on these Saturday nights that I will never ever forget. After my usual sneaky-peep to see who was coming through our front door, I climbed back into my bunk bed, (the top bunk was mine, Pru, my sister, never had a choice which bunk she preferred, as the midwife said 'this one will push her way through life, no matter who gets hurt along the way'. That top bunk was mine and that was that, she had no say in the matter, bad girl Gaynor). As I was just settling down to sleep, I heard a strange loud noise coming from the back garden, I peeped through the curtains and, to my surprise, there was a hoofing great big horse. My God, I have gone stark raving bonkers, how can I possibly have a nervous breakdown at my age, I thought. Maybe I fell asleep and was dreaming, I rubbed my eyes, went back under the covers and endeavoured to go back to sleep. I realised I could not go back to sleep, for I was never asleep in the first place, so I looked out of the window again, just to make sure, and there it was standing on the grass making that strange noise, yes, it really was a horse. I wasn't going mad at all. It turned out it belonged to one of my brother's women-friends. I can understand if she would have brought her dog with her, but a horse totally confused me.

I recall one Saturday night I woke up to use the toilet and found myself struggling to see. Normally the landing light was left on, for I did not like the dark. As I tried to find the light switch I went into a panic and could not breathe properly, I was terrified. My sister also woke up and the pair of us were trying to get some light in the house, we called for our brother who was supposed to be looking after us, but he was not in the house – he had gone out and left us on our own. Standing at the top of the stairs crying, scared out of our lives, we thought the bogey man was going to come and get us. What added to the terror was that the electricity meter had run out and we could not find the emergency coin which Mum and Dad would normally leave on top of the meter in case it run out – it had gone. At the age of seven, my mum and dad packed my sister and me off to Nan and Granddad's house as Mum was going into hospital to give birth to her sixth child. My memory is very vivid at this stage of my life and I recall running out in the middle of the night in my nightie crying for my parents. I felt scared and alone, something happened to me inside the house. As much as it pains me to say, I remember being in the bathroom and my Granddad was there with me. All I know is that he touched me in an inappropriate way, that's when I must have ran out of the front door riddled with fear. Ever since that night at my Nan and Granddad's house, I felt dirty inside and that somehow I was to blame. I remember filling my underwear with mud and leaves from our back garden and walking around like this. I feel that this was my way of trying to express how I felt about myself and that I wanted someone to notice, but I don't think they ever did. Every Wednesday my grandparents would come to our house, which I dreaded. I recall my Granddad always used to make me sit on his lap, which I did through gritted teeth. Later on down the line I discovered that what happened to me was sexual abuse. It affected every area of my life, especially in my relationships with men, and gave me major issues with intimacy, not just with men, but with most people who came into my life. After this episode, I must have suppressed this memory so deep down inside of me that as I got older, the memory did not exist. I had disassociated myself from this completely, not having any awareness of what actually happened to me. But what did remain within me and was very much present and on the surface, were the subsequent feelings and effects that seemed to grow with me as I grew up. It never went away. I do believe that because of what I experienced that night at my grandparent's house, subconsciously, I felt that I was not loveable and was a bad person, therefore I attracted men who treated me badly and disrespected me.

Chapter Two

Little Mum

My Mum gave birth to a baby boy called Brady when I was seven years old. During this time, my elder brothers must have left home, for there were only three kids in the house alongside our parents. Mum spent most of her time at home washing nappies and attending to this little person who could only scream and fill his nappies with this ghastly smelly stuff. When my brother, Brady, joined the family, I seemed to grow up almost overnight. I began to take on many different roles, not the kind of roles one would expect from a child of seven. These roles I was playing out were not optional, I became a victim of circumstances as I witnessed my parents' decline.

On many occasions during the night, I found myself in my parents' bedroom attending to my little brother, who was screaming his little lungs out, which when he cried, I cried. I had red eyes constantly for some time when he was a baby. Mum, for some reason unbeknown to me at the time, did not seem to stir, neither did Dad. As time went by, I realised that something was not right or 'normal' inside the walls of our home, especially on those Saturday nights. One of my roles, along with my sister Pru, was to be the baby-sitter for little Brady. Sometimes I felt like he was my son, not my parents'. I seemed to spend a lot more of my time taking care of him, changing nappies, and staying up half the night rocking him to sleep than they did. When Brady was tucked up in his cot and my sister was asleep, as tired as I was, I could not go to bed and sleep. I would be looking out of the landing window waiting for Mum and Dad to come home from the pub. I could tell when they had turned into our street for I had done this so many times that I got to know the sound of the engine of Dad's car. My heart would start pounding and my body would be absorbed with fear of what would happen after Dad had parked his car, which was nowhere near the kerb like other cars down our street were parked. Mum would be hanging out the door before Dad even had time to turn his engine off. On one occasion, I saw Dad trying to help Mum walk towards the house, to my amazement, one minute Mum was there, the next minute she had disappeared. Then I realised that she had fallen over the wall and ended upside down in the bush in the front garden. Dad had just left her there and walked into the house. Naturally, I took on another role as The Rescuer; help was on its way. Down the stairs I flew, out the front door and I pulled Mum up and out from under the bushes. I had to move quickly for fear of the neighbours seeing us. Mum was always very sensitive when it came to appearances and the thought of someone in the street having a view of Mum's legs sticking out from a bush, would have mortified her, regardless of having 'the best legs in Ruislip' which she always quoted, especially when she was intoxicated. Mum did have very lovely legs and I could understand her wanting to put them on display, but in a more dignified and stylish manner.

This experience with the incident with Mum in the bush, was not a one off. My parents spent a lot of time in the pub and very rarely when they returned would they either be sober, merry, happy or enjoying each other's company. Occasionally they would return seemingly carefree and joyous, but oh how quickly that disappeared. I could never go to sleep until Mum and Dad came back from the pub, for I knew what was going to happen. It almost became a routine, a repeated pattern which I came to dread, especially on those bloody Saturday nights. The minute they came through the front door, my body dived out of bed and would go to the fourth step. I did not have to count them, for I was so used to sitting on that step which, for me, became the step from hell.

The needle would hit the record and at high volume, the merry-go-round of madness would begin. By the time I reached thirteen, I must have been the only child around to know all the words to so many songs dating back to the roaring forties. I knew all the songs that were out during and after the Second World War: Glen Miller, Vera Lynn and especially, Frankie Vaughan. My Dad had a great voice and would put a hat on and hold a stick like him and sing on the 'microphone' *There Must Be A Way*, which was one of his favourite songs. He sang with such passion and devotion looking into my mother's eyes with tears of emotion in his. It was like they were the only two people in the pub, in fact the world, he adored and cherished my mother and she him.

Getting back to the step from hell, the music belted out and I could hear Mum and Dad singing along to the music for hours. I sat on that step feeling cold, tired and agitated. I really wanted to get tucked up in my bed and sleep but I daren't because I knew, at any minute, I would hear the scrape of the needle being dragged off the record, then all hell would break loose. Voices would be raised, getting louder and louder, and then I would hear the sound of glasses and other objects being thrown around. At this point, my backside would leave the step and I would hover nervously outside the living room door. I knew what was coming, Mum and Dad would be exchanging words, not very nice ones at that, calling each other names that I did not understand, but I knew they were not words that people would use when they were happy. Mum would scream 'HELP!' That's when I, The Rescuer, had to get to work quick smart, for Dad was hitting Mum and my job was to get them apart. There would be blood everywhere, it was like a horror movie and a war all wrapped into one. How I managed to yank Dad off Mum I will never know, for Dad was a well built, strong and stocky man with strength beyond belief. On one occasion I found myself in an ambulance that I had called when I raced down to the phone box, for we did not have a phone in those days, I was still in my brushed nylon nightie and had nothing on my feet. This situation became the norm for me, the police were often called to Wingfield Way and most times they did not even ask where I lived, for they had been to our house so many times before, especially on those Saturday nights that they recognised my voice. Mum had a gash on her forehead – Dad had obviously clobbered her with something. It was terrifying to see, me holding her hands and trying to reassure her she will be okay, even though deep down, I thought she was going to die. They stitched mum up and home we came.

The next day, I would come down stairs rubbing my tired eyes which were red from crying. I hardly slept as a child; I was always too frightened to go to sleep on the nights my parents were out down the pub. Dad would be standing in the kitchen cooking breakfast and Mum would be hanging out washing or pottering around the house doing something or other. You would never, in a million years, have believed that these same two people who loved and adored each other were trying to kill each other the night before; not a word was spoken about this.

Mum used to say, 'We don't discuss what goes on in our family with anyone.' This was my first lesson in dishonesty, denial and superficiality. I started to pick up traits which I adopted from observing my parents' behaviour, and was already learning, at high speed, to wear different masks for various different situations, to disguise what was really going on behind them.

I looked forward to Sundays, this was the only day that it was almost guaranteed that my parents would not be in the pub. Dad would bring us all breakfast in bed, placed on a tray with a little rose in a glass, which he would pick from the back of our back garden. He planted this rose bush himself, the smell of them was beautiful. My day was full of simple pleasures; I would merrily skip down the stairs and assist Dad with the roast dinner, which I looked forward to every Sunday. We had fresh mint growing in our garden and dad would send me out there to pick some for the mint sauce. I remember him chopping it up with some vinegar and sugar, sometimes he would let me have a go, and this made me feel very important indeed. Come dishing-up time, my sister, brother and I would fight to get to the kitchen to get to the prized saucepan of Mum's delicious white sauce to go with the Sunday roast. We would push and shove each other – it was chaos, all over a little scraping of sauce left in the pan before mum washed it up. After dinner I would go to my room, my little safe haven and wait for the top twenty to come on the radio.

I loved my music, it took away my loneliness. I found that if I listened to music, there was always something in most songs that expressed how I was feeling, that I could relate to, for I had nobody who I could talk to about my feelings. Music was my comforter; I could go anywhere I liked in my mind whilst listening in my room. On Sunday evenings my parents, sister, brother and I would snuggle up round the open fireplace. Dad would put a slice of bread on a fork close to the fire to toast it, then we would have beef dripping on the toast with salt and pepper; I loved it. My Dad would give me money to sit behind him in his chair with a back scratcher; he loved his back being scratched. When night was drawing in, I would fall asleep on his lap and he would pick me up and place me in my bed where I had a blissful night's sleep, which was very rare. I guess I knew there would be no kicking off during the night as Mum and Dad would retire to bed sober.

My first day at infant school was a day I will never forget, Mum waved my sister and I off outside our house, still in her dressing gown. I don't know why she didn't take us on our first day, but off we went with our little duffle coats done up, satchels hanging over our shoulders. In the picture that was taken of us that morning, I looked like a little boy because Mum had cut off my beautiful long wavy hair. It broke my heart; she did this because I used to scream when she was combing the tangles out of it. I remember my teacher told me to 'sit down son', when I realised it was me she was talking to I went bright red and told her, 'I am not a boy I am a girl!' I was so nervous and scared that I wet myself and my pee was trickling down my leg on to the floor. I wanted to run, but could not move for I was gripped to the seat with fear.

On my first day at secondary school, I felt pretty similar to how I did on the first day at infant school, the only difference was that now I was eleven and extremely damaged emotionally and mentally. Pru, my twin, was the clever one out of the pair of us. I was told on many occasions by Mum that I was thick, which did not do much for my self-worth and self-esteem. I had no sense of who I was. I had no identity whatsoever, which was down to the numerous roles I had to play growing up. The first time I was called 'thick' was when my family were at Heathrow Airport waiting for my eldest sister to arrive from America. I needed to go to the toilet badly. Mum pointed out where they were but when I got there, one door said 'male' and the other door said 'female', I was confused, I did not know what I was. I ran back to Mum, nearly wetting my pants, and asked her what I was. My family laughed until they cried, but, for the life of me, I couldn't work out what was so funny. Mum told everybody how thick I was. This became a standing joke for many years to come.

Standing in the playground on that first day, I had another terrifying experience – the teachers told us to stand in lines where we then would be allocated to our classrooms. There was no way I was going to be separated from my sister. I clung onto her like a sinking ship; they would have to literally pull me apart from her. We were given a test paper to assess our ability in order to put us into sets, ranging from 'A' – the highest to 'E' – the lowest. When the results were called out in front of the whole class, my heart pounded so fast that I thought it would come flying out of my chest. My biggest nightmare was just about to happen. My sister's name was called out, she was put in to set B, eventually my name was called out but, by this stage, I was in the middle of experiencing my first ever real panic attack: my mouth was all dried up, I could not breath, I was drenched in sweat and thought I was going to faint through hyperventilating. All I remember was that the letter D being mentioned, straight away I thought yeah that's about right, D for dunce. Then to add salt to my wound, I realised that this meant I would not be in the same class as my sister. We were going to be separated. I was going to be left alone with all the other dunces in my class.

After a term or two went by, all the pupils seemed to end up in the same class regardless what level we were at by this stage of our schooling. Great news for me I thought, I can be with my intelligent sister now. I could never concentrate at school and had no interest whatsoever in any lessons besides P.E. I loved sport and netball was one of the few things that I found I was really good at.

I schemed up a plan in my sneaky devious little mind. I was the gobby one, the one who would put on a front and not show my fear, especially when confronted with the school bullies. I remember my dad always told me, 'Even if you're terrified, never show it.' That stuck with me then and still remains the same today. I made a deal with my sister; in fact she had no say in the matter as usual. I told her that I would copy her work in exchange for being her body guard, if anyone picked on her, I would deal with them, for Pru was pretty timid in comparison to me.

I have never forgotten one particular day at school. All the pupils were sitting in the assembly hall as it was exam day. My God, I tried everything in my power that morning to try and get out of going to school. I even went to the extreme of raiding the fridge to find leftovers from the dinners that Mum would keep in the fridge for bubble and squeak. I found some peas and carrots and scarpered up the stairs heading for the bathroom, knowing Mum was in her bedroom and could hear me. I made that awful retching sound that people make when they are throwing up and emptied the peas and carrots down the pan. Mum came flying in the bathroom, she stood there with her hands on her hips and nodding her head and said, 'not that old stunt again Gaynor.' Obviously this was not the first time that I had tried to pull the wool over Mum's eyes to get out of going to school, especially if my sister was ill. Some days I would hide in the shed all day until school was finished and then come in as if I had been at school all day.

Anyhow, getting back to the day of exams, I kept nudging my sister to whisper the answers to me; it was so quiet in there that you could have heard a pin drop. The teacher was pacing up and down, keeping an eye out for anyone who might have been cheating. It was the last minute of the exam and I had managed to get quite a few answers on my exam paper, when, all of a sudden, the teacher yelled out my sister's name. Whilst my sister was telling me to pack it in, for I was pestering her throughout the exam, the teacher came over and ripped her papers up. Poor Pru, oh well I think I passed with flying colours! I'm sure they thought she was cheating.

I hated school so much. I was terrified of teachers and, in fact, I was terrified of everyone, especially any figures of authority. I dreaded going to school, but dreaded going home even more. I could not concentrate during my lessons for my mind was fixed on what I was going home to. The fear of what might be waiting for me when I got home was so intense that I had to sit down halfway home from school in the launderette until my panic attack subsided a little. By now, panic attacks were a regular occurrence for me. By the time I reached the top of our road, the tears would start; I felt so lonely and frightened and wanted to run away, for I was still not mature enough to understand my emotions. I always feared that I would be locked up in a lunatic asylum for the rest of my life. I was so mixed up and confused. When I entered the house, the smell of smoke and alcohol nearly knocked me over. It was like walking into a public house; there sat Mum and Dad and these strange looking barflies that my parents brought back from their afternoons drinking down the local pub. I would run up to my room, my little sanctuary where I felt safe, well, as safe as I could be.

Chapter Three

Daddy's Girl

I was Daddy's girl and Pru was Mum's favourite, or so I thought. I worshipped my dad, I simply idolised him and him me. He always made me feel worthy of being loved, thank God, I don't think I would be here today if it was not for the love he showed me. I was a real handful when I was growing up. I would answer my mum back every time she had a go at me; it seemed like I got the blame for everything, even though I was not guilty the majority of the time. I stole ten pence out my mum's purse one day and Dad took the blame for it. Mum did not speak to him for a day or two over that. Another time I stole a box of chocolates that Dad had bought for my mum. I scoffed the lot until I felt sick, and then shoved the empty box under my bed. I was rumbled and Mum said, 'she is so thick, she did not have the intelligence to even get rid of the empty box properly'. Now it was programmed in my brain and I truly believed yes I am thick. When you get told something so often about yourself, especially when you are young, eventually you can end up actually believing it's true.

During the Second World War, my dad fought for King and Country and spent years as a Prisoner of War in a concentration camp in Germany. When I was little, and Mum and my siblings were asleep in bed, I would go in my dad's bedroom (at this stage in my parent's relationship they had separate beds in separate rooms). Dad would sit me on his knee and tell me what he experienced and witnessed during the war, which was excruciating to hear. Dad was mentally, emotionally and physically damaged by his experience. He told me about the time he tried to escape from the Prison of War camp with his best friend – his friend got shot and Dad carried his dead mate over his shoulder. My Dad had been shot a few times but managed to survive, thank God. The pain on my dad's tear-soaked face broke my heart. He told me how he witnessed thousands of Jewish people, men, women and children ,all queuing up thinking they were going into the showers; they were terribly mistaken, they were going in to be gassed to death. Dad saw the dead bodies being carted out of there, after anything of any worth was stripped from these poor helpless people. How can anyone recover from seeing that? Well, as I mentioned earlier, Dad never did. He returned a broken, traumatised man with deep insecurities. He was so possessive with my mum. When drunk, Mum could be very flirtatious which would arouse Dad's jealousy and result in Mum getting numerous amounts of 'good hidings'. Mind you, she gave him as good as she got.

My Mum married my dad when she was sixteen and, looking at the photographs, you would think they were two movie stars. My Dad was terribly handsome and my mum was absolutely stunning. I could write so much just on the romance between them, especially in the early days when they met. But their marriage tragically deteriorated and although I couldn't understand it at the time, I understand today that it was the result of two people who were the victims of King Alcohol. I hated the stuff; I had seen what it turned my parents into. It eventually destroyed their marriage and caused destruction all over the place.

My world fell apart the day I came home from school and saw my house surrounded by police – they were everywhere. I saw my dad being carried out of the house by six police officers and thrown in to the back of a police van which looked like a cage inside. I kicked two of the officers and screamed for them to let go of my dad. I was unaware, at that time, that Mum had been to court to get a restraining order to prevent Dad coming anywhere near her and the house. He obviously broke this, so was carted off to the police station.

I must have been twelve or thirteen when my parents broke up; it was one of the saddest days of my life, regardless of the hell I went through with the drinking, violence, emotional neglect and all the other consequences of being raised in a dysfunctional environment. You would probably think I would be relieved they broke up, but no, I was devastated. What was I going to do now they had taken my daddy away? Who was going to stick up for me and carry me asleep to my bedroom and tuck me in? Who could I talk to in the night when I could not sleep? I spent so many nights with just my daddy, we would talk and talk and often Daddy would make breakfast at four in the morning. I was happy when it was just me and Daddy.

My younger brother, Brady, was fortunately too young to remember much of the ups and downs of our parents' turbulent marriage. He was spared the experience that I had but then he never really had a chance to know our Dad. I cannot imagine how he must feel, even to this day, to be the only one out of six siblings who has no memories of his father. He has listened to Mum and the rest of the family speak about Dad all his life. It must have been torture for him. In fact, to be honest, I have seen how badly it has affected him in so many ways in every area of his life. There were questions that he desperately needed answers to for he has heard so many different versions from so many people that it left him confused, frustrated and extremely angry, which in his shoes, I would be too. Dad was a man who had so many different sides to him. His sense of humour was endless, he had so much love in his heart, he was talented in so many ways, a perfectionist in his work as a painter and decorator; he was such a proud man. However, Dad had a temper on him which was not pretty. He was definitely a man not to be messed with. He was one of the hardest men in Ruislip, and everyone knew who Norman Goodchild was. My Dad was a strange mythical character to my little brother. Watching the torment and pain Brady is still going through breaks my heart. Brady has so many of our Dad's qualities, especially his heart – he has a heart of gold and, like Dad, he would give you his last penny. He also would punch above his weight, even out of his depth and, like his Dad, he never backs down.

As far back as I can remember, I felt lost and lonely, riddled with fear and completely inferior to everyone I came across no matter who they were. I felt misunderstood; my emotional needs were never met, I had no encouragement, praise or reassurance. I spoke but no one seemed to listen, I was trapped inside a bubble, totally detached from the world outside of it. I was constantly light-headed and lethargic throughout my childhood. I totally withdrew from the world and the people in it. I was totally alone. It was so bad that Mum took me to see a psychiatrist a little while after Dad was carted off. I recall this strange-looking eccentric type of man sitting at his desk; I trembled with fear as I lowered myself on to the chair. He was asking me all sorts of ridiculous questions, like 'Have you got a boyfriend?' Have I got a boyfriend I thought, you silly little man, I lost my virginity underneath the miniature railway track at Butlin's Holiday Camp before I even turned twelve but what has that got to do with anything? I couldn't remember the details or even how old I was when I lost my virginity, but I couldn't see why it was relevant.

I was aware Mum and one of our neighbours were pacing the floor outside the consulting room, eagerly awaiting my diagnosis. How the bloody hell could this doctor help me? I refused to tell him anything for I was programmed to keep quiet and say nothing about what went on in our house. The poor man had no history to work with so it was a complete waste of time, which I knew it would be before I even arrived at the hospital.

Now Dad wasn't living in the house anymore, things had to change rapidly, for it was just me, alone, against the world. I had to protect myself. I was not that little girl anymore, I had to think and behave differently. My defences were up, and a wall appeared around me, solid like a rock. Firmly set in my mind, I reflected back on what Dad told me. 'Show no fear, even though you're terrified.' I wanted to take the world on like he did. My preparation was taking place, on came my imaginary shield, and weapons. My attitude was my greatest weapon. My hair was cut short and spiky and dyed bright orange; I had razor-blade earrings and razor blades round my neck, this might have had something to do with the latest craze at that time when Johnny Rotten and the Sex Pistols were storming the charts. Yes I was a punk rocker, which suited me down to the ground, for they were wild and aggressive with the attitude of not giving a fuck, just like me. I was becoming a complete menace to society. Other kids in the street were playing knock down ginger (where you knock on someone's door and run away), but this was too lame for me. I threw a brick through one of the neighbours' living room windows as they sat there watching the television. Boy did I run – I was a fast runner, in fact the second fastest runner at junior school. I hid behind the small wall next to our front door. Flying towards our house, came the woman whose window was smashed with the brick I threw. As she hammered on the front door and Mum appeared, I was trying hard not to laugh for Mum thought I was at a school disco, well, that's what I told her. When the old bag said she saw me running away, Mum was having none of it and defended me. All was going well until I coughed and that was it, and I was caught. I got a right telling off, and a slap around the head. Mum often slapped me round the head; even if it hurt I would never show it. As time went by, I become more rebellious and filled with rage, I was furious about everything.

If my memory serves me well here, I believe Dad went to prison at about this time. I remember a letter he wrote to my mum. It had Pentonville Prison on the paper. Dad said that Butlin's, (which was what he called prison) was not very nice this year and he would not be going back there again. I missed him terribly and he must have been missing all of us too.

Chapter Four

The Intruder

One afternoon there was a knock on the front door and, having a strop on about something or other as usual, I opened the door. There stood this man with teeth that looked like they all were trying to escape out of his mouth at the same time. He had a mop of ginger hair and was skinny as a hairpin. He asked to see Mum. Mum introduced me to him, Rob was his name. I hated him on sight and gave him one of many of my *what the fuck are you looking at* looks. When Mum introduced me as Gaynor he gave me a strange look, for I found out later he thought I was a boy. This was the second time in my life that I had been confused with a boy. It was understandable though, because I dressed like one and acted like one. Looking like a male was part of my defence. I believed that if I let a fraction of femininity slip, it would come across as weakness and that was not going to happen. I was constantly reminding myself that it was me against the rest of the world, Dad was not here to protect me now, and had not been since that awful day when he was taken away from me. I was livid when I realised that this mere excuse for a man was actually dating my mum. WHAT? Not a hope in hell if I can help it. This man came into my home where my dad should be, and to make this whole scenario even more excruciating, wait for this, he was only twenty-bloody-one – (eight years older than me, and twenty five years younger than Mum). I'm dreaming, I thought, I'm imagining this, I must be, this can't be real. But once I realised this was, my mission was to kick his pitiful back-side back to where ever he crawled out from. I knew I had my work cut out here but found that I was not alone on this occasion for once. My siblings, especially my brothers, were not whistling Dixie themselves with this new man in our Mum's life. Between us we endeavoured to make his life a living hell.

I recall on one occasion, I can't remember which brother it was, but they were chasing Rob and, God knows how, he ended up on the roof of the house, terrified to come down. This man really did not have a clue what he had let himself in for with the Goodchild family. Even the most mentally, emotionally and physically strong person on this planet would struggle to sustain their sanity in our family unit, especially if they were not welcome (and that's not including our Mum, she was in a class of her own). Mum, like Dad, was not someone to be messed with; Dad taught her nearly everything she knew, she had a very good teacher.

Rob tried everything he could possibly think of to win my affection. He gave me and my twin a record player for our birthday, well I'll tell you what I did with that, I launched it through the air directly at him and told him to F-off! I observed how he was worming his way into our home. I was mortified when I came downstairs one morning to find him stretched out on our couch, he stayed all night. I marched upstairs, straight into Mum's room to have a serious word with her. After the onslaught and exchange of words, I knew I had wasted oxygen, mum was not budging on this matter and I had that awful feeling that she had no intention to, ever.

CHAPTER FIVE

MY NEW BEST FRIEND

Mum and Rob got closer as the months went by and it was not long before he was sharing Mum's bed. I cannot describe the resentment I had towards him. One day, when they were out, I found my eyes staring at an eggcupful of scotch whisky in the bottom of the bottle which was next to the settee where Mum always sits. I hated alcohol for the devastation that it caused my family; I knew that the liquid in the bottle had caused Mum and Dad so much trouble but I was inquisitive. Before you could say 'vicker's knickers' I grabbed the bottle, dashed to the downstairs toilet and downed it. The minute that liquid hit my throat and made its way down to my stomach, I had the most amazing feeling I have ever experienced. For the first time in thirteen years I was transformed instantly, from a young girl who had no confidence, full of fear, hopeless and distraught, into someone with self-esteem, self-worth and confidence. I was relaxed. It felt like someone had opened the door of the bubble that I had been trapped in all my life and set me free into a brand new world. I wondered why my parents did not feel the way I did when they drank as I just did. This was it, I did not need my armour that had been weighing me down anymore, I had found something that I had been searching for all my life up until this point; it was the answer to all my prayers. This magical substance called alcohol became my best friend, my comforter, my everything and the memories of what this substance did to my parents was a thing of the past. Now this bird was about to spread her wings and spread them out as wide as she could . . .

When Mum returned with her toy boy, it did not take her five minutes to notice that the remains of her bottle of scotch had disappeared. I knew she would not think for one minute that I was the culprit, for she knew how much I hated alcohol (on this occasion it was guaranteed I would absolutely be in the clear). Unfortunately for me, my little secret was soon discovered.

On New Year's Eve, Mum and Rob were going out for the evening to celebrate. As they were making their way to the door, Mum yelled out, 'don't touch the wine.' I don't know why she said this, for she knew how much I hated alcohol. Within a few minutes of them leaving, I had downed a bottle of red wine and was on to my second. I remembered how I felt from my first experience of alcohol and I wanted those wonderful feelings to return again. The next thing I remember was someone carrying me up the stairs. I could feel everything spinning round and the next minute I was pebble-dashing the walls with vomit all the way to my bedroom, where I remained until 2 p.m. the next day. As I slowly swayed down the stairs feeling like death on legs, I was greeted to a choir chanting 'don't let me die'. Apparently I repeated these words over and over when I was being lifted up the stairs by the dreaded toy boy the night before. The thought that I had been in this man's arms made me feel like throwing up again, for I would not have been an inch near him as a rule. After this incident it did not take Mum too long to put two and two together and realise who stole her scotch, I had been sussed.

From the day when I first got acquainted with my best friend, King Alcohol, my mother's new relationship didn't seem such a big deal as it had at the beginning. I had bigger and better things to occupy my mind now. My life had turned a corner, so I thought then, for the better !

Despite being well underage to be frequenting in the local public house, one night I thought I'm going to pay this place a visit. I was well aware that it sold alcohol, for when I was growing up I spent many afternoons and evenings outside the pub, nose pressed up against the window witnessing the slow transformation of my parents. The more they drunk, the more awkwardly they were positioned at the table. I always knew when Mum was drunk, for her head would drop to one side and one of her legs would be bent at the knee, resting on the other one with her skirt slightly rising up. It was the same with Dad, when he was ten sheets to the wind his left eye would slightly close like he had developed a squint. Anyhow, it was my turn now. On came the make-up and the high heel shoes to make me look taller. Dressed to kill, I went in and made a beeline to the alcoves right at the back of the pub. Bizarrely, it was designed to a western theme, with the swinging wooden doors that went both ways. The only thing it lacked were cowboys propping up the bar and a few horses outside. As I discovered later on, just like the Westerns I had seen, this place had proper bar-room brawls, especially on Friday nights. There would be chairs, tables, glasses, bodies, the lot all flying through the air.

I mingled with some people I knew from school who were a little older than me and the drinking began. For obvious reasons I could not get the drink from the bar myself. Firstly, I had no money, and secondly, I could not take the risk of being caught drinking UNDERAGE. The last thing I remembered from my debut encounter was being frog-marched out and being told 'You're barred.' I was drunk as a lord on Cinzano and lemonade and a few halfs of Skol lager. My drinking habit increased very quickly and, by this stage, I was smoking grass as well. I became the life and soul of the party and very popular, especially with the lads. Whenever there was a party it was guaranteed I got an invite. By now I was wild and an outrageous flirt. I very quickly worked out how I could use my sexuality to manipulate and control whoever I wanted to get whatever I wanted. I was never short of a boyfriend. The men loved me and the girls hated me, as I was attracting far more attention than a lot of the other girls in the pubs and at parties due to my flirtatious manner. I could also consume a large amount of alcohol and had won many competitions drinking the men under the table. I loved the attention I was getting, it was so new and I craved it so badly growing up.

I was becoming aware that drinking was occupying my mind more often than not. I noticed that I was always the first to arrive and always the last to go at parties. I also seemed to be the only one standing and could not understand why others were passed out or putting their coats on to go home, when I was just warming up.

I must have been about fourteen by now, my memory is very patchy, it is not a selective memory where I choose to remember certain things and disregard others (I wish this was the case, for things would or could have turned out rather differently in my life). My memory is what it is and I have no control over what is logged inside my head. My life was spiralling out of control and I was barely going to school. I played truant most of the time and caught dysentery which was a nasty stomach bug that was sweeping the schools in the area. It was bloody awful, what was so degrading about this bug is that for months samples of my faeces had to be taken and tested in the lab. I also spent a lot of time going back and forth between doctors. I frequently had giddy spells and it turned out I was anaemic and had to take iron tablets for a long period of time.

★★★

I suppose you're wondering what happened to my father. Writing this makes me feel so very sad, even though this was a long time ago it was a very significant phase of my life. I missed my dad terribly; not a day went by when I did not think of him.

One day I received a letter from him, his address read, 'Third bench on the right, Ruislip Gardens Park'. My Dad was homeless and sleeping on a park bench. My heart bled for him, I was devastated. He spent most of his time drowning his sorrows in a pub and became a chronic alcoholic although, looking back, I suppose he had been for years. He had lost everything: his wife, family, home, work – the lot. Dad eventually got a flat in Northwood and I would spend as much time as I possibly could with him, it was heartbreaking. He was still helplessly in love with my mother. It was gut-wrenching to see the decline in my father's health. He suffered severe rheumatoid arthritis and had terrible trouble walking. His flat looked so clinical; it was so cold and uninviting. He would have Marvel dried milk on the shelf in the kitchen, which shocked me for he loved a good cup of tea with his breakfast. There was hardly any food in his fridge; it was soul-destroying remembering the roasts he used to make. There stood the love of my life, reduced to a mere shadow of his former self. He told me that he spent many evenings walking the streets and looking in the windows watching families sitting all together, eating, watching television, laughing and enjoying each other's company, thinking to himself, I had a house, a wife and a family once. My father looked like he was the loneliest person on this earth.

Looking back, I wish I knew then what I know now, and had maturity on my side, I could have been a lot more use to my father back then. I may have been a lot more mature than most girls of my age, but that was down to the fact I had to grow up quickly to survive my childhood, I had no choice. As I mentioned before, I did not spend much time at school and now that Dad had his flat and was in such a state, I decided I was not going to school anymore. I would leave my house in the morning, naturally Mum thought I was going to school, but I went straight to Dad's and returned home after school hours had ended. Eventually, I started bringing four or five friends round to Dad's which Dad loved, not only was he happy to spend time with his daughter, but he enjoyed the company of my friends as well. We used to bring big bottles of cider round, which Dad did not mind. I remember one day my friends and I were at Dad's as usual and there was a knock at the door. Dad said 'Quick hide!' There were bodies under the bed, in the wardrobe, we hid in any nook and cranny that we could fit into. We did not find it that funny when we heard the truant officer talking to my father at the door. 'I know they are in there,' he said and said he wanted to come and look inside. My Dad was having none of that and, as the truant officer put his foot in the door to stop my dad from closing it, we heard one big clump, it was the truant officer, Dad had knocked him clean out.

CHAPTER SIX

DON'T LEAVE ME DADDY

I met my first proper boyfriend (excluding the numerous one night stands) at the school disco. He was a guitarist in a band that was doing a gig at the school the evening I met him. I remember him sitting on his motorbike outside the school waiting for me to come out the gates. I felt like I was the cat's whiskers as he handed me my crash helmet and we zoomed off down the road on full throttle, drawing even more attention to myself. I found myself spending most of my time at his house. In comparison with the insanity that was going on in mine, his house appeared to be 'normal'. I was not used to 'normal' I was used to chaos and all the upheaval that takes place in a dysfunctional family environment. The way things took place in my boyfriend's house were predictable. Meals would be served at the same time each day; there would be regular intervals for mugs of tea and always a biscuit with it, chocolate ones at that. Mum used to think that she was being clever in our house when I was growing up, she would buy chocolate digestives and turn them upside down so that they looked like they were plain, so the kids would not eat them all. She also used to put butter in the margarine tub and vice versa, so I thought I was eating butter and all along it was margarine; I hated it. It did not take me too long to work out what was going on but I never let on that I knew. I got the sense that the pupil was starting to take over the teacher!

As I said, my boyfriend, Michael, and I spent as much time together as we could. It was bliss not being in my house with all the goings on there. He proposed and the engagement came around quick; we were to be married the day I turned sixteen. With a sparkling ring on my finger, I was the happiest I had ever been. Michael took me out for a drink one evening, even though I was still underage. After a few gin and oranges a very different Gaynor appeared to the one he knew. He had no idea of my shenanigans with my wild parties, drinking and one night stands, I think he thought I was a virgin. He started to get concerned at the speed I was knocking the drinks back and demanding more. Michael was not a big drinker and did not touch drugs; he didn't have any awareness of alcoholism and drug addiction or the behaviour that went with it. In comparison to all the other men I have had in my short life, he was very different, not the kind of person I would normally choose to associate myself with.

I must have been with my fiancé for well over a year and we were almost inseparable. I had let go of the friends I used to kick about with, for now I was all grown up, so I thought, and going steady. My Dad had been introduced to Michael and took an instant liking to him. He could see he was a sensible lad, but nevertheless, Dad gave him the verbal going over which was really embarrassing. Dad looked him straight in the eyes and said 'If you ever hurt or lay a finger on my daughter, I will break every bone in your body.' Poor Michael was quivering with fear. Then Dad put out his hand to shake his and I have never seen anyone so relieved in the whole of my life, he thought he was a dead man.

Dad had managed to find himself a lady-friend, he met her at a divorced and separated club, I remember that night as I came with him. Looking at my dad, then looking me up and down the guy on the door thought better of asking me my age, for Dad had that look on his face, the kind of look you would not challenge, so in we went. Not long after meeting this lady that night, they married. All I knew about this lady was that she and her husband had split up and, after the divorce she found herself without a roof over her head as her ex kept the house. There was something about her I did not like. It wasn't that she was a threat to the relationship I had with Dad, I just sensed she was after somewhere to live and knew Dad had a flat and was vulnerable.

School was coming to an end, well it never really got started for me, the little amount of time I spent there. I remember a gang of us piled in to the local with signatures from friends scribbled all over our white shirts. Amazingly, we were served alcohol, I guess the publicans were not that concerned what your age was back in those days, as long as money was going in the till, that's all that mattered.

Mum was getting on with her life with her toy boy and dad was enduring married life with his new wife. I knew and understood at this point that Mum had moved her boyfriend in on the rebound after she split with Dad, and that Dad married his wife not for love but to spare himself the loneliness and isolation that he had endured for so long. I could see he was not happy and never would be again without Mum in his life. His wife was cold and heartless and the complete opposite of Dad. He needed warmth and comforting, especially being the broken man he was since the divorce from Mum. To be honest, I have no memory whatsoever attending his wedding in the registry office. I know I went for I have seen photos of me there, but have no recollection of that day whatsoever, I must have been paralytic.

After leaving school, I started looking for paid work, as I had to pay for my keep. Finding a job back then was easy, not like it is today. It did not matter if you were skilled or not, you could drop out of one job and find yourself in another the next day. My first job was working in a travel agency in Ruislip, Middlesex. I was terrified the first day at work as I had very poor communication skills, as I had never learned to communicate without the need to shout and wail to be heard. My typing skills were average but I was not well travelled, the furthest I had been from home was the Isle of Wight. I had no experience of any countries outside the UK. My boss could not be bothered to train me so I really had to try and work this out myself, but to no avail. I ended up stamping holiday brochures in the back office, I could not really screw up here, could I? Yes I did, after stamping hundreds of brochures with the travel agency's name on it, I realised that I had stamped them upside down. My boss was, by now, losing his patience with me and realised it had been a mistake taking me on (I totally agreed with him there). One morning, when I came through the door, sluggishly as normal, he told me not to bother taking my coat off as I was going to the American Embassy in

London to pick up the customers' visas. I had never been to London on my own before and was terrified. I managed to find the Embassy and remember hanging around for five hours waiting for the visas to be processed. By the time I got back it was well gone six and I was greeted by my boss with his hands on his hips accusing me of skiving as I was so late. I was bloody furious, skiving? I had been hanging around most of the day waiting for the visas. He ordered me to get in the back office and start stamping the brochures, the right way round to make the time up. That was it, I told him to stick his brochures up his arse; that was the end of that job.

My fiancé was waiting outside the travel agency when I came storming out. To top it all, he also questioned my whereabouts in those six hours I was waiting for the visas. By now I was raging, I had not seen this side to him before and, without hesitation, I claimed that our engagement was well and truly off and we were over. I felt no sadness, absolutely nothing, it was like I had never even known this man, never mind being engaged to him – it was like we never existed. Considering I had been in this relationship some time, it may appear strange that I decided and accepted that this was the end of our relationship. It is not as though he had done something terrible that justified me ending this so abruptly. I feel that I was not happy with him trying to control me and tell me what to do – he was not my father. My barrier came up just like it did in my early teenage years.

During this short period working as a so-called travel agent/ brochure stamper, I have to stress that my father became sick and ended up in hospital. After work was finished, I would go to the hospital to visit Dad, bringing him his favourite biscuits and Jamaica ginger cake. I noticed Dad had lost weight and he seemed to be disappearing rapidly in front of my eyes every day. That horrible hospital smell was dreadful. It smelled like a combination of Dettol and something rotting, it made me feel ill the minute I stepped foot in that awful place. One evening, when I reached the ward where Dad was, I had the shock of my life: there laid a man who I worshipped and idolised, he had a long tube with a bag hanging outside of his bed; it was filled with some kind of fluid, which turned out to be urine. It was a catheter which I did not understand at that time. My Dad must have weighed about nine stone at this point. Being a well built stocky man, to see him with his skin hanging from his bones and eyes bulging and staring vacantly into space broke my heart. I did not know what was happening to him. He was moved from Mount Vernon Hospital to another one further away, by now I was frantic with worry. I remember walking into the ward once and his wife appeared by his side, which was a novelty as she had not bothered to see him much when he was at the other hospital from what I can remember. Dad was in a wheelchair and asking her for his cigarettes, which she refused him. She really was a bitch. I was right about her all along. I asked one of the nurses what is wrong with my dad to which she replied he has a cyst on his brain. I did not know what a cyst was back then and did not question her any further. Dad got transferred back to Mount Vernon Hospital and lost even more weight; he was a shadow of his former self.

I will never forget this day as long as I live, I came up to the hospital as I did every day since Dad first got admitted. I poked my head round the ward and looked in the corner where Dad's bed was. As I bent over the bed to kiss and cuddle him in the way that I always greeted him, something was different, something was terribly wrong. My Dad did not recognise me as I shook his frail body repeatedly saying my own name – no response. Dad was out of his mind on something, he muttered the word 'sausages' for he could smell them. One of Dad's favourite foods was sausages, he recognised the smell because it was meal time and the food trolley was being wheeled round the beds serving up the patients' suppers. The nurse heard Dad's feeble, quiet muddled request for sausages but it was totally ignored. That was it, the straw that broke the camel's back. First my dad does not recognise his daughter that he adored, and secondly he was denied food. Something was happening to him and I was not going home without an answer, I was beside myself with worry, worry being an understatement.

I marched into a room outside the ward and saw a nurse sitting at her desk, I sat myself down and, holding back the tears, I demanded to know what the hell was happening to my father. With her face as cold as ice she said 'Okay, this is what's wrong with your Dad, he has a brain tumour and will most probably not make the night, he is going to die.' *Going to die*, I could not believe what my ears had just heard. I hazily got up and returned across the corridor to Dad's ward. I took one look at him and I remember mumbling the words to him, 'They said you are going to die,' with that I passed out with shock.

My memory of this horrendous, most pain-staking time in my life is very patchy. All I remember was making my way across the road to the bus stop repeating out loud to myself that my daddy is going to die, I vaguely remember laughing out loud which must have been shock.

It was a Saturday, the day I was told this devastating news about Dad. I had been going to the hospital every day since Dad first got admitted and, on the Sunday, I was round my friend's house in the morning talking to my friend about Dad. Looking back, not only was I still in shock but must have gone in to total denial for I decided I was not going to the hospital to see Dad that day, I would go the next day. Tomorrow never came, there was a knock on my friend's front door where my brother Max stood there looking very sad. He told me Dad had gone, my God, my dad had passed away all alone and I was not with him. This news was to be the start of my journey into self-destruction.

Standing in the hospital's chapel of rest accompanied by my family and Dad's wife, I looked at this figure which was laid out on the bed with a white sheet up to his neck with just his face exposed – my dad. He looked nothing like him, his nose seemed pointed and his skin was grey. I watched Mum kiss Dad's forehead and others saying their goodbyes. Mum mentioned my name which pulled me out of this trance-like state. She asked me to kiss Dad goodbye, I looked at him but could not comprehend what I was seeing or what was happening. I could not bring myself to kiss my dear Father goodbye.

I vaguely remember leaving the hospital and the journey home, my head could not handle the reality of all this. I ran as fast as my legs could carry me, round the block laughing hysterically, looking like someone who has just escaped from a mental institution. I had lost it.

I do not have much recollection of how I was feeling in the days leading up to Dad's funeral, yet again the only emotion that I can identify was fear. Dressed in a black skirt and top, sitting in the hearse with my twin, eyes fixed on the car ahead with my dad in a wooden coffin, was like watching the scariest horror film only I seemed to be playing the main role.

Sitting in the pews in a little chapel in the cemetery where Dad's coffin was placed on a table, I heard a voice say 'as Norman Goodchild lies here...' and that was enough for me. I could not believe any of this, I let out one high pitched scream followed by uncontrollable sobbing. I believe I was taken outside screaming for my dad, I was inconsolable. The congregation left the chapel and were making their way to the piece of ground that had been dug up for my dad, down with the worms and other creatures that live below. After prayers and passages were read out from a bible or something to do with religion, I watched in complete bewilderment, as they lowered my dad into the ground. My brother Max and I were the last to leave the grave, we both stood there holding each other gazing down at that wooden box with our Dad in.

Yet again I have no recollection of the journey back, for all I knew was that I was now totally alone. My family and the rest of the mourners celebrated Dad's life in the tradition that we were familiar with, yes, in the local pub which we took over entirely that day. All the Goodchilds together under one roof, it was mayhem. As the drinks kept coming, we became louder. We were working our way through every song dad used to sing and all the songs he loved. The last thing I remember of that day was being carried out of the pub. I was intoxicated up to the hilt.

Chapter Seven

Out of Control

The local pub had become my second home for I spent most of my time there getting drunk at every opportunity I had. Being without alcohol was too painful; I could not live in the reality of life without my father. I associated myself with people who drunk as hard as I did. I would sit up at the bar surrounded by barflies talking gibberish and nonsense to pass the time. I hooked up with a man who was a lot older than me. He worked abroad most of the time but on his return to England he would come into the pub loaded with a wallet full of notes and a big stash of mind-altering substances. It was not long before I started dating him. He became my candy man, I could have any drug I wanted and most of the time did not have to pay for them, I couldn't anyhow, for I did not have an income at this time. Unlike today, women did not pay for drinks when in the company of a man. Equality was not an issue back then and it was expected of men to buy the ladies a drink, which suited me just fine. What I had to my advantage was youth, a well-proportioned figure and my outrageous and flirtatious mannerisms. Loaded with all these pulling qualities, getting someone to buy me a drink was easy and I knew it. Most nights I spent in the pub I was off my face, talking a hundred miles an hour, hyperactive (which was down to the handfuls of speed which used to be called 'blues' back then which heightened your senses and gave you a feeling of euphoria). Running on an ego that constantly had to be boosted to make me feel wanted, loved and accepted. I had to be the centre of attention whenever I was out, it was something I craved and was hungry for, to be noticed.

I had a lot of tools installed in my mind when I was growing up. These tools were coping tools which helped me to overcome uncomfortable situations. They also were used to control and manipulate people, to hurt and confuse, to get what I wanted, to put on different masks and disguise the real me (whoever that was, for I had no identity due to taking on so many different roles as a child). I adopted this behaviour by observing others, including my parents. I was too young to know any better. I would boost men's egos and tell them how handsome they were. They could have been the ugliest person in the world but it was a way of being for me and I lied so much that I began to believe a lot of my lies were true. I was so superficial. I could only feel from my head, not from my heart, but I was not aware of this at the time. I really believed the nonsense I came out with.

I became aware that I seemed to be hanging out with, and dating, men who were much older than me because I was looking for a father-figure and trying to find my dad in all of them. Inevitably, none of these men matched up to my father, on realising this, I dropped them like hot bricks.

The months passed so quickly after Dad passed away and my life was so painful to live. I missed and longed for him constantly. My Dad died thinking that I was happy and in love with Michael, even when we split up, I did not tell Dad, for I knew how much he worried about me. He would have turned in his grave if he knew the way I was behaving, especially with the men and how I was disrespecting my body with what I was putting in it and using it as a weapon to get what I craved so much – to be loved and cared for. I was very mature for my age at sixteen but also vulnerable with deep insecurities and fear of being abandoned. I thought about dating a barman, that would suit my needs, all round–free drinks, which basically I was getting anyway, drinking after the pubs had thrown the punters out at closing time. I put my plan into action and before long I was not only seeing different barmen, I was living upstairs with one of them, fantastic, so I thought, living in a pub what more could I ask for? Most nights I stayed up drinking with the bar staff and a few of the heavy drinkers who put a lot of cash in the tills and were invited to stay on drinking. The punters were happy and so was the landlord, until he got so drunk that people were going behind the bar helping themselves. The landlord was actually losing money rather than gaining, especially when we would knock up different concoctions for cocktails experimenting with different spirits and so on, we must have cost the brewery a fortune. Back then we did not have computerised tills like we have now, they were the old fashioned ones where you had to push down hard on the numbers and press another one for the till to open. It always made that 'ting' noise when you slammed the till back in.

I soon started working, or should I say helping out, behind the bar, huge mistake on the landlord's part for I could not add up to save my life. My mathematics was pitiful, I was confused enough when trying to do sums with pen on paper, never mind trying to add up the rounds of drinks in my head. In the end I gave up, I would tell the punters after all the drinks were served 'Forget it, have it on the house.' I became the most popular barmaid overnight, couldn't see why ! Unfortunately for the punters, their free drinks were short lived. One morning the landlord said they were having a stock check. Oh dear I was in huge trouble now, they are going to be hundreds down, for this went on most evenings when the pub was heaving for there was less chance of me being caught out. After the stock check, the landlord made a beeline for me and, to put it mildly, he verbally assassinated me so I was demoted to the other side of the pub and continued to do what I do best, get drunk, take drugs and screw up.

I am ashamed to admit that I got a kick out of drawing men in until I won their affections, then dropping them without a thought of how much I hurt them. The chase was much more fun than the actual catch. Men were like toys to me; when I wanted to play, I would pick one out, have my fun and then put them back in the toy cupboard. I left a trail of broken hearts behind me. I hurt men so badly that two men tried to commit suicide after I left them (fortunately they were not successful). My behaviour and how I treated men when I was actively drinking alcohol was a different story when I had sobered up. When the reality set in of how terrible I had been, the feelings crippled me. I felt overly remorseful, riddled with shame and guilt. I was disgusted and loathed myself. I couldn't bear to think of how much pain I had inflicted on these men. Little did I know at that time, but in the future I would get back what I had given out. I truly believe in Karma, what goes around comes around, as you will see further on down the line.

I know I am painting a really horrible picture of myself here with the way I have treated people. But I survived a lot as a child: the baggage filled with negative emotions, not having any self-worth or self-esteem or even a sense of who I was. Adding alcohol and drugs on top of all these feelings turned me into what I became. Underneath all of the bravado and ego tripping, I remained a nervous, sensitive and damaged little girl who would not hurt a fly. All she wanted deep down was to be accepted and to fit in.

I had now reached a stage where I could not go anywhere or do anything without reaching for the bottle. I would find every reason and excuse to justify my drinking, If you had a childhood like mine you would drink or if it's raining, or next door neighbour's budgie had fallen off its perch. I could not go to job interviews without having a few glasses for courage and would only seek work that fitted in around pub opening hours – nothing was going to get in the way of my drinking. I remember when the bell would ring for last orders in a pub, my heart would start racing with fear of where I was going to get the next drink from. From my first ever drinking experience, I noticed that I always would come to with a hangover. Not the normal type of hangovers where your head would hurt, take a tablet and all is well again. No, mine were physical, mental and emotional. My body would shake the minute I opened my eyes, mentally I would be heavily depressed and emotionally, I would be overcome and absorbed with crippling unidentified fear, remorseful, bewildered and swallowed up with agonising guilt and shame. I knew something was terribly wrong with me, how different I was in comparison to others. I knew my drinking was different to how most people drank and feared for my sanity.

It had been three and a half months since Dad passed away. They say time is a healer and I know it was still early days, but every day was getting harder to get through, the pain and the loss I felt was getting worse, totally unbearable, even when I was drunk (which was most of the time) the alcohol and drugs could not take these feelings away.

CHAPTER EIGHT

NOT FIT FOR THE JOB

One spring morning in March 1980, I was woken by the landlady of the pub shaking me and telling me to get downstairs for an urgent phone call. When I put the phone to my ear it was Mum. All she said was 'Go and get a nice dress on, I am getting married today'. I thought it was a joke, the phone was slammed down and back to bed I went. Minutes later, I got woken up again – same thing, 'Your Mum's on the phone,' I heard the landlady say. At this point, I was not amused. I am not the happiest of people first thing in the morning. Mum repeated the same thing again to me. When I realised she was serious, my response was, 'You must be effing joking,' with that I went back to bed and crashed out. I was informed later on, on that diabolical day, that others knew about Mum getting married to her toy boy, but it was all hushed up as Mum was frightened I would go ballistic if I found out. She knew how much I resented the fact that she had replaced my father with a mere excuse of a man and how much I loathed him, I would have pulled out all the stops to prevent this hideous marriage from happening. I also found out that the landlord and landlady were attending the wedding and that they knew all along and had organised for the wedding reception to be held here in the pub where I was living.

Totally slaughtered throughout the day, I found myself downstairs at the wedding reception. Obviously I did not give Mum and my so-called stepfather my blessing, but I got stuck in to the free booze that was on offer. As time went by, my stepfather being with my mum was not so much of a problem for me. Now that they were married, I had to let go of the resentments and anger I had towards him. Mum had made her choice and I felt it was time to move on. My stepfather did try his best to fit into the family and I have to give credit where it is due, he kept bouncing back and taking it on the chin when he was criticised for making a decision or trying to put his stamp around the house. My relationship with my mother changed a lot since Dad had passed away, I was beginning to realise that she also had a life to lead and that if my stepfather made her happy then I would try and be happy for her. Even though my mother had a lot of pride, we would sit down from time to time and talk about her feelings and what it was like being married to another man after she had divorced my father. I was beginning to understand that she had to do what was best for her and what made her happy. I was beginning to become aware that there are always two sides to every story.

★★★

My twin sister and I took two different paths as we grew older. Pru kept herself to herself. I feel that even though she was raised in the same household as me, it affected her very differently to how it affected me. The only way I believe Pru coped with the dysfunction of our childhood, was to let it all go over her head and dissociate herself and the memories of it all. I feel that this was not a conscious way of being for her, I believe it was an inbuilt coping mechanism that helped her survive it all. I may have got this wrong, but this is how I see it.

My eldest sister Diane spent many years flying back and forth to America. She eventually married an American who was in the forces, and settled in the UK. I started to get to know her more when I was in my twenties. Looking back in hindsight, it would have been nice to have had her around when I was growing up, I most certainly could have done with her support. I can understand why she left home as soon as she could, for her childhood could not have been easy either.

I had been out of work for a while and decided that I needed to get off my backside and earn a living. My luck was in when a friend of mine mentioned there was a vacancy going next door to the pub in the Express Dairy; they were looking for a secretary to work in the warehouse. The position would entail sorting out and checking the spread sheets, a bit of typing, filing etc. It could not be that difficult, I thought, sounds pretty easy. The first thing that sprang to mind was that I knew where I would be spending my lunch hour, in my local pub next door, how handy, I thought. Another bonus, in fact a huge bonus, was that I was the only female working in this department alongside twenty or so men who worked in the warehouse below my office. Having an ego as big as mine, and thinking I was the centre of every man's universe, I was in my element. The morning of my interview, I paid special attention to my appearance. I carefully chose an outfit that would draw attention to my assets, so to speak, bearing in mind that I was also going to be interviewed by a man, so naturally I would use all the resources that I had mastered to a fine art to draw this man's attention, so he would overlook the lack of experience I had in this field of employment.

Checking myself in the mirror ten or so times, pouting like Marilyn Monroe and trying out all my various expressions, I picked out one that I normally use to reel in my prey. With everything present and correct, I knocked back a few large vodkas and off I went.

I entered the warehouse to be greeted by a choir of wolf whistles, which obviously stimulated my ego, and made my way up the stairs and knocked on the door. There sat a man who must have been in his early fifties. He looked creepy; there was something about him that made me feel uncomfortable. He took me through the formalities and I over exaggerated my experiences. After giving me the once over, I could see he was far more interested in my appearance than any competence that was required for this position. The job was mine if I wanted it.

I was now living back home with my family, this felt rather uncomfortable for me, especially as I had been running free and doing whatever I wanted to do, especially with my stepfather there. I did my best to try and get on with him, if not for his sake but for my mother's. I had started my new job at the dairy but I was still partying hard every evening and big time at the weekends. My alcohol intake was increasing at a high rate and so was my drug taking. Every morning when I turned up for work, I was either still drunk and high or suffering a huge hangover. My boss woke me many a time when I dozed off with my head on top of my typewriter. One afternoon at work, my boss called me over to his table and asked me to pick some paperwork up from the floor. As I bent over, his hand slapped my back side, my natural reaction was to knock him clean out and, to make it worse, I noticed that *The Times* newspaper that he always seemed to have his head buried in was a smoke screen – he was really looking at pornography magazines, the dirty old bastard. My first instincts regarding this man the day I came for my interview were spot on.

As time went by, this vile little man's behaviour was getting progressively worse and the day came when I had had enough and decided to take action to get him fired. I spoke to my union rep and proceeded to get the ball rolling. Unfortunately my case was dismissed, for it was my word against his and, obviously, he denied all the allegations that were made by me and therefore the case was closed. I was not going to take this lying down and decided to have words with the lads in the warehouse. After a very long lunch break down the local, we decided that everybody who worked under this despicable man was going to down tools and go on strike until he walked. This now was becoming a serious matter, there was going to be all sorts of problems now, the delivery drivers were out of action, the warehouse packers had downed tools, everything came to a stand-still and it was great. All these men were on my side and doing all this for me, wow, did I feel the big shot or what?

The strike was short-lived, other dairies were being affected and chaos broke out, people were panicking and yes victory had been achieved, the old bastard got fired. I was the talk of the dairy; it was marvellous. Things were very different now at work and, to my horror, my old boss was replaced by the union rep himself. Now I had to tighten my belt and knuckle down to doing some proper work, for falling through the door in the mornings still sloshed from the night before, crashing out on my type writer and having long dinner breaks had to stop now. My new boss very quickly cottoned on to how incompetent I was and there was no way I could bluff my way out of this now.

There was a meeting arranged for all the bosses and big noises from other express dairies to attend a huge conference here at the depot where I worked. I was asked to come in early and set the table in the conference room, serve the tea, coffee, nibbles etc. It was also requested that I dressed smartly and act becomingly. Okay, I thought, not a problem, I can do that. The night before the meeting was to take place, I was at a wild party high as a kite on weed, speed, and drunk as a lord, with no thought of the next day and how important it was with the big conference taking place. I woke that morning, not in my bed at home, I was still at the house where the party was. I noticed the time was ten o'clock, shit, I should have been at the meeting hosting it. I had no time to go home and get changed, so straight to work I dashed. I was still drunk and high from last night's events. In I crashed through the doors, hair uncombed, face looking like Alice Cooper, my make-up was smudged all over my face, and to top it off, I looked down at what I was wearing, to my horror I had a T shirt on with the slogan in big letters which read 'Please ignore anything I do I'm pissed.' Oh my God, I could not even talk properly, I blurted out 'Anyone for a drink?' and with that, fell over crashing into the table. I certainly do not do things in half-measures, this was to be the end of my career in the dairy. I was fired on the spot, (didn't understand why).

As I was unemployed again, I thought that I would have a little break before seeking work again. I played hard all day and all night, in and out of relationships, propping up the bar, and sitting there talking to anyone who would listen and became the bar's agony aunt. I would listen to men moaning about their lives and give them advice and sort all their problems out for them. It was a good way of avoiding the reality of what I was feeling and the mess I was making of my life. By now, I was totally hooked on speed and loved the highs, but the comedown from this drug was terrible. It was like a huge dark cloud weighing heavy on top of me, the depression was excruciating, I was taking the drug as often as I could now to avoid the inevitable terrible, uncontrollable panic attacks, the hot and cold sweats and the overwhelming depression that seemed to go on forever when I stopped taking drugs.

Reflecting back to this time in my past, I have some really happy memories, especially down my local pub. My friends and I would have fancy dress nights, our crowd was always organising some event or other. On a Thursday night there would be a singer called Dave Cook, who would sing and play his guitar. We were like his little fan club, we loved him, and he loved the attention. We knew every word to every song he sang, The Beatles, James Taylor, I was in my glory as I mentioned before, music was my first love, my company when I was alone, I lived for my music and still do today, but for different reasons now, simply because I enjoy it.

One of my friends, who was part of the gang, was working as a care assistant in an old people's home in Harefield. There was a vacancy and she put in a word for me. An interview was arranged and I got the job. There were a few snags with working in Harefield. The hours were long, sometimes the shifts started very early in the morning and I had to get two buses and then walk from the village down the country lanes to the home. There would be twelve hour shifts which put the mockers on my drinking which I was not pleased about; I had to work most weekends, which I lived for. The wages were really good and after paying Mum for my keep I still had money for clothes, going out, drink, drugs and managed to save a little as well.

Working in this residential home which was run by the council was an eye-opener. It was heart-breaking to see these helpless old people being dumped in these homes. I would see them arrive on their first day and watch them go downhill rapidly. Being moved out of the homes that they had lived in most of their lives, uprooted and put in a new environment where they felt lost, alone and afraid, was often too much for them. I saw many die not long after they have been admitted, they gave up. Only a few had their faculties and most were incontinent. There was a sick bay where the residents who were senile had to be constantly monitored at all times. It was so depressing to see, it was more like a psychiatric hospital than an old people's home. There were residents who would wander off in the day and night, who would eventually be found wandering around in the grounds, sometimes half-naked and covered in their own faeces.

There would be screaming and shouting, crying, someone waiting by the front entrance with their little suitcases packed wanting to go home. It makes me sad thinking about these poor old people. I had always said that I would never want ever to be put in an old people's home. I'm not saying all old people's homes are run badly, but this one I worked in was, it was atrocious. The man who ran the home was an alcoholic. He would sit in his office drinking from a large bottle of coke, which I found out later that it was filled with whisky. He was a horrible man with no compassion whatsoever for the elderly, he was a brute.

I was still drinking heavily and would pop a handful of amphetamines before I started work, so that they would kick in by the time I arrived. They would give me a false sense of energy. You have never seen so many beds made so quickly in all your life. It sounds terrible that someone like me looking after old people was high on drugs. I was in control, I know this may sound like denial or a justification, but I have a heart and genuinely cared about those people. Mind you, my patience was tried and tested to the max whilst working there, I would have used incontinence pads thrown at my face and I even had to lift this ninety-something woman into the bath single-handedly, even though I was advised not to do this alone. I could not see what harm a fragile old lady could do to me. I soon found out, I was the one that ended up in the bath; she was as strong as an ox.

I saw many dead bodies there. Part of my job was when someone had passed away was to wash them, put coins on their eyes and close them if they died with their eyes open. Then I would see them put in a plastic zip up bag and taken away. So sad.

Getting into work was becoming a struggle by now, especially when I was on the early shift, so I decided to hitch-hike on the Victoria Road one morning. I had no trouble getting a lift, even though I would get strange looks from the locals seeing me stagger along the kerb with my thumb hanging out. I would arrive to work in the most stylish of cars. Rolls Royces, sports cars, you name it, I arrived in it, and it was great fun. I would spend my lunch hour in the village pub, knocking back as many drinks as I could before

I went back to work. My friend and I would take it in turns having a kip on one of the resident's beds, while the other kept a look out. One day I awoke to find my boss leaning over me, I was instantly dismissed, but managed to get my job back for I was good friends with the union rep.

My job became more bearable when we had the painters and decorators in. The antics my friend and I got up to with them! She would be up to no good with one of the workmen and I was no better myself – this went on for months. Another time the fire alarm went off and the fire brigade were called. We were assisting the residents to get out of the building and doing a head count. My friend went missing and was later found having it away with one of the firemen. My God we were a right pair, we were insatiable.

I had been working at the home for a year or so now, the hours I was putting in and the partying was really taking its toll on me. I was still grieving for my father terribly, he never left my mind, and time was still no healer of mine.

CHAPTER NINE

WRONG SIDE OF THE COIN

I was drinking down my local one night when I noticed a piece of paper had been thrown down beside my feet. When I picked it up, it read 'call me', when I looked up I saw this man sat there with his arms draped round another women, I thought what a cheek, he wants my number, yet he is already with someone else. Foolishly enough, I put the piece of paper in my pocket. In hindsight, it was the biggest mistake of my life, which you will come to know. Around this time, I also met a man who played the guitar in a band, we hit it off immediately, he had these large brown puppy dog eyes and a big mop of black curly hair, and he was so cute. He was travelling and lived in a caravanette whilst working as a welder and gigging around the country. I spent many nights cuddled up to him, gazing at the night sky happy in love. It was the first time I had experienced these kinds of feelings with a man, for he was different to most men I had dated. He was kind, soft and gentle, romantic and would cook me romantic meals and end the evening playing his guitar and singing me love songs. The only problem was that he was married and lived in Stoke on Trent.

One night I bumped into that man whose number I foolishly kept. I could tell he was a lady's man, considering the way he introduced himself that night. He was all over this women and was giving me his number discretely. The red light should have come on for me that very night I first met him, if he could do this to her then he would do the same to me, but being so vulnerable and emotionally unstable, I ignored the warning signs. I was playing a dangerous game for I was seeing both men at the same time, why I pursued this relationship with the womaniser I really cannot tell you; I was happy and contented with the guitarist. Maybe I could not handle 'nice', bearing in mind I was not familiar with contentment, therefore I would subconsciously jeopardise anything good in my life. The time came where I had to make a decision as to who I was going to stay with out of the two of them. I could not make my mind up, so in the end I tossed a coin, heads for the guitarist and tails for the womaniser. The womaniser won, I cried as I said my goodbyes to Mr Nice Guy.

After the pub had thrown us out one night, I decided to take my new boyfriend back to my house, I knew Mum would be in bed and I could sneak him in for a while. I crept in the house and nearly jumped out of my skin, there was Mum sitting in the darkness with a large drink in her hand, she was pretty worse for wear. Mum never suffered fools gladly; she knew I was hiding something or someone. She stood up with her hands on her hips and yelled, 'Come on and show yourself, what are you, a man or a mouse?' Sheepishly, Rob appeared but as he held out his hand to shake hers, Mum pushed it away and told him she did not like him, she also added she would not trust him as far as she could throw him. Mum has always been a good judge of character, and had a lot of wisdom for her years, not often was Mum wrong. Ooh, I wish I had listened to her, she could see right through him.

Rob was living with a friend and occupied a room in his house. One night when he asked me to come back with him, there were naturally, a few things that I needed to ask to get to know him better. Being a good few years older than me, I assumed he most probably had been married and had children. He denied ever being married and having kids which I did not buy. When he crashed out that night, I went searching for clues, scouring through his drawers to find some evidence there. I came across some photos of two young boys who looked the image of him. I approached him the minute he woke and he apologised for lying. What he also kept from me was that he was still married and was separated from his wife (who I later discovered was still living in the matrimonial home a few doors down the road from where he was lodging). The evidence was there right in front of me from day one, this man was nothing but a liar and a cheat but I stayed with him regardless and gave him the benefit of the doubt.

Since I had started dating Rob, I came off the drugs which I had been addicted to, for he was anti drugs and I had to make a choice, him or the drugs. I managed to put the drugs down, but increased my alcohol intake to help me cope with the withdrawals. Desperate to leave home, I agreed to find somewhere for us both to live. We rented a room in a flat which his friend was buying. Throughout our first year together, living under the same roof, I started to discover what kind of person this man of mine was. He liked his booze and we spent our time drinking in the local, which was fine in the beginning, for he drank like I did, at least we had that in common.

I would wake up most mornings lying on a mattress saturated with urine, he had wet himself which became a nightly occurrence. You would think he would feel embarrassed in the morning, but he had no shame whatsoever. He also was extremely possessive, in the beginning I was flattered for I thought it was just because he loved me so much, how wrong I was there. It got so bad that in the end I was terrified to bump into any man I knew, for if I said 'hello' I would be accused of sleeping with them. To try and avoid upsetting him, I would walk with my head down, hoping I would not be recognised. I nearly died of embarrassment one evening, we had been drinking in the pub most of the day and night and went for a meal in a nearby Chinese restaurant. It was packed solid being a Friday night; we managed to get a table and ordered our meal. Not long after it had been served, I noticed a guy who I recognised a few tables away and was filled with horror. I nearly had my head in the food, for my head was dipped down so low, hoping he would not see me and say hello. The next minute I heard this loud voice shout out my name, damn, I had been spotted. Shaking with fear, I tried to explain to Rob that he was a friend of a friend, which was true, but he was not buying any of it. The whole of the restaurant downed tools as they turned to see what all the commotion was all about at our table. Rob was screeching at me, accusing me of all sorts, I wanted the carpet to swallow me up. The next thing I knew, he had got my plate of food and emptied the plate over my head. There were strands of chow mein hanging off my eyelashes, sweet and sour prawn balls sitting on my head and special fried rice everywhere. With that, he got up and walked out the restaurant leaving me sitting there. What made it worse was I had no money of my own to pay for this meal I never got to eat. The manager of the restaurant approached me and offered me a few napkins to try and clear my face of food; I explained I had no money, which she was fine about. She sat down beside me and said 'He bad boy' and asked me to hold out my hand, she read palms and told me to run away fast, 'He no good for you,' she said, which was rather obvious after what she and the rest of the people in the restaurant had just witnessed.

I was so desperately unhappy and yet I thought I was in love with this monster of a man. I was so needy and insecure before I met him and whatever identity I thought I had was now slowly slipping away. We eventually decided to buy the flat privately off of his friend, that's when things got progressively worse. Rob never wanted to stay at home in the evenings and do something normal like cuddle up and watch TV, he had to be in the pub. He worked as a printer on Fleet Street and earned good money. We could have lived comfortably on his wage, plus I was still working in the old people's home. He managed the financial side of things, paying the bills, mortgage etc., but somehow we never seemed to have much to show considering what we had coming in.

I left the old folks' home and Rob asked me to marry him. I was nineteen years of age and, like a fool, I said 'yes', the wedding was going to be a secret for if Mum got wind of it, she would hit the roof (the irony). I only told my brother Max and his wife who were to be our two witnesses. We were married in Uxbridge Registry Office and spent our honeymoon in a guest house in Devon; he really pushed the boat out here, for with the money he earned we could have had a luxurious honeymoon abroad. Travelling on the train, loaded up with a crate of lagers, I sat there like I was going to a funeral, not a honeymoon, and this should have been the happiest day of my life. I had little affection shown to me, which I was in desperate need of, I just wanted to be loved. I felt so lonely, and lost, still longing for the love of my father.

The first night of our honeymoon I got a punch in the face. It was the first time Rob had hit me; I had done nothing wrong but was accused of looking at a man. We only stayed a few days in the B & B for my husband had wet the bed and he decided to cut the honeymoon short and leave without paying. What a start to married life. He would not let me go out with friends or family, I could drink with him down the pub that was about it. We argued constantly and on many occasions things would be thrown and smashed when he lost his temper. If his food was not cooked exactly when he wanted it, it would be thrown at the walls. I spent my time cooking and washing, Rob would not eat food that was reheated, no matter what time he came in, I would be expected to cook for him. My knuckles were red raw from washing. He was so tight with money; he would not buy me a washing machine and made me wash everything by hand.

One night Rob came in early hours of the morning stinking of booze, he would drink in London after work in a drinking man's club so he said, God knows what he was doing when he was not with me. I pretended to be asleep when he came through the door. I could tell he was angry and could hear him muttering under his breath. He was in the kitchen and I could hear him in the cutlery drawer; I could have sworn I heard him say he was going to kill me. With my body trembling and sweat dripping off my brow, I tried to keep still when he approached the bedroom. I felt something press hard down on my back, as I sat up the bed was covered in blood, he had stabbed me. I ran to the bathroom terrified. Rob went to sleep and I stayed cowered in the corner with just a towel wrapped round me until morning.

The bleeding had stopped and I could see in the mirror there was a large gash across my back. I should have gone to the hospital and had the wound stitched up. He did not apologise the next day, he behaved like nothing had happened. No one knew about this, if my family had found out, my husband would have been a dead man. The predicament I was in had now ground me into the ground, I was suicidal. I tried to cut my wrist open in front of my husband, hoping he would change and show me some affection, but obviously this did not work, he picked me up and threw me outside the front door and slammed it behind me.

It was a well known fact, everyone knew what Rob was like and how he treated me, they were aware of the severity of his temper. Even a friend of my husband who had known him for years begged me to leave him, for he had seen what he had put his first wife through.

I had no coping skills whatsoever. I could not handle any of my emotions, I never could, I was never shown how as a child and I did not want to be abandoned again. The thought of being abandoned like I was when my father left home filled me with fear and despair. I had no fight left in me; this bastard had drained me of everything. Not only was I starved of affection, he also rejected me sexually. I remember crying on many occasions and begging him to cuddle me, he would laugh and tell me how pathetic I was.

I was totally faithful to my husband, which was a complete turnaround considering the person I was before I met him. After years of torment and abuse, I decided that, seeing as I was constantly getting accused of cheating, I might as well go ahead and do it, what have I left to lose?

Rob was working a night shift and would not be home until the early hours of the morning, so I decided to go for a drink and get back a good few hours before he came home. That night I met someone and brought him home with me at the end of the evening, one thing led to another and we ended up in bed together. To be honest I was not comfortable and felt pretty awkward about the whole thing and decided he had to get dressed and go. Just as he was about to put his clothes on I heard the key go in the door and in walked my husband, he had finished work early. I grabbed the guy and his clothes and shoved him in the wardrobe, I threw myself under the duvet and pretended to be asleep, and my heart was going ten to the dozen. This guy only had to cough or sneeze, that would have been the end of me. That poor man spent hours in that wardrobe, his bladder must have been ready to burst considering the amount of booze we put away in the pub. Rob got up to spend a penny, with a minute to spare, I let this poor guy out and shoved him out the front door, this was the closest I had ever come to death, and was spared by the skin of my teeth.

I had been married for three gruelling years by now and felt that life had let me down, along with all the people in it. I was still trying to make this monster love me, I could not let go. I became obsessive of his every move for I always sensed he was being unfaithful to me. I noticed scratches on his back and semen stains in his pants. When I challenged him, I was laughed at and told to f-off as usual.

One afternoon before sleeping off an afternoon drinking session, my husband told me to wake him an hour before the pub opened, to give himself time to wash and dress, this was the normal procedure when he was off work. I had been to the well-women's clinic which I was referred by my doctor. I had been suffering from depression which progressed not long after my father died and was accelerated by the abuse I suffered from the minute I got involved with my husband. The doctor said my blood pressure was high and my menstrual cycle was all over the place, so it was suggested I went and got checked out at the clinic. The nurse asked if I could be pregnant, fat chance of that I thought: for one, I was on the pill and two, my husband hardly came near me, if he had then I must have been drunk or asleep. I could not remember the last time he made love to me, well, had sex with me I should say. I had a pregnancy test done anyhow. On this day I had returned to the clinic to get my results. My husband was not aware of the test and obviously did not notice my depression, what did he care? He had not got over the love affair he had with himself.

Chapter Ten

My Baby Speck

The nurse came straight out with it and announced I was pregnant. I couldn't be, no, it's a mistake; I had never thought of having children, emotionally I was still a child myself. I walked out of the clinic numb, but a thought came to me that this could change things – if I have Rob's child, surely he will change and love me. I walked through the front door, went straight in the bedroom and woke Rob up. I told him I was going to have his baby and waited for that arm around me that I longed for for so long. To my horror, he turned round and yelled, why are you waking me up telling me this, f-off. Not long after that, he got up and went down the pub. I stayed at home sobbing my heart out.

I decided I was going to keep this baby no matter what. Rob's attitude to the announcement that I was pregnant had changed, but not for the better, he doubted being the father and had no interest whatsoever. I went to the ante-natal clinic alone; nothing had been bought for my baby for he kept hold of the money we had to live on. I spent most of my time alone, if not working he would be getting drunk in the pub. One day he told me to go to the job centre to get work, in fact he frog marched me there himself. He picked out two jobs for me, I did not want either, one of them was to work in the bakeries in Ruislip which meant I had to get up extra early for the buses did not run at five-thirty in the morning and I started at six. I had to walk a good few miles to work and being pregnant did not help matters. On my first day I was asked to put on my uniform – my God it was hideous. I had a green puffed sleeve blouse with an apron to wear over it and a green hair net. I looked like something out of *Alice in Wonderland*. I could not be seen out the front of the shop in this, I would die if anyone recognised me. I had only been there a couple of days and had had enough already. One morning I was putting the cakes I had just creamed out on display in the front window when I noticed my husband and my younger brother staring through the window nearly wetting themselves with laughter. That did it, I asked my boss if I can take an early lunch, went out the door never to return again.

I was four months into my pregnancy, my sanity was hanging on by a mere thread, and still Rob was showing no interest in my pregnancy. He was so cold, heartless and evil. How could anyone be so cruel especially in these circumstances?

I managed to get a cot, some Babygrows and things from a couple that Rob knew – they only wanted a hundred pound for the lot, which begrudgingly he coughed up the money for, it must have killed him to put his hand in his pocket. He also put up a couple of shelves and painted the so-called nursery blue! Was he assuming I was having a boy, who knows what was going on in his warped little mind?

During one of many visits to the hospital for my scans, I mentioned to the nurse that I had not felt a movement from the baby, all I experienced was sickness and heartburn throughout these four months. I became a little concerned as they kept changing the dates when the baby was supposed to be due which should have been around August. My blood pressure was extremely high and the nurse said I look pale and unwell. Not surprising, if only she knew how I was being treated by my husband. I was still on the receiving end of his drunken rages and all the abuse that went with it. He had the audacity to send me off for an interview working in a factory cleaning and packing pieces of steel and lifting heavy boxes. I tried to hide my pregnancy at my interview which I succeeded and got the job. The work was hard and was taking its toll on me; I could not go on much longer, I felt so ill and exhausted. Eventually my boss noticed that I was heavily pregnant and I was asked to leave and not return. He was horrified to see a pregnant women lifting large boxes of steel from one place to another, he kept nodding his head in disbelief as I headed for the door.

Rob hit the roof when I returned home, ranting and raving about money, he could not have cared less about my health and that of our unborn child, till this day I still wonder how he sleeps at night.

One morning I had woken up feeling so ill – I could hardly get out of bed I was so weak. I sensed something was wrong and went to see my doctor. I was seven months pregnant now and still had not felt any movement hardly from my baby. The doctor took my blood pressure which had gone through the roof. He told me to get myself to the hospital immediately. He wrote a letter and told me to give it in when I get to the maternity department. I went home, put a toothbrush in my bag and off I went to the hospital. I was put on the ward with all the other mothers-to-be. My eyes filled with tears watching the proud fathers-to-be entering the ward with flowers and bits and pieces they had brought up for their wives. I kept my eye on the door hoping and waiting for my husband to walk through it, for I had left a note for him to explain what had happened. He decided to show his face about ten o'clock that night. He arrived empty handed, I could see he had been drinking and showed no concern whatsoever. He was more interested on keeping his eye on the clock on the wall, for he did not want to miss 'last orders' at the pub, he only cared about getting back to the pub on time. My blood pressure was constantly monitored and I was having scans every day, for they could not give me a date for when my baby was going to arrive.

My mum appeared one morning with my sister's partner, she was worried sick. I explained to her about my blood pressure and reassured her that I could go home once it had gone down. What I did not tell her was that I did not want to go back home, it was that bastard of a husband and his treatment of me that had been the cause of my raised blood pressure. I never wanted to go back to that flat again. I was so withdrawn from the world and the people in it, I felt mentally ill as well as physically drained. I was right back there in that bubble again, the bubble I was in when I was a young girl. Lonely and isolated, cut off from the world around me. My mind was slowly shutting down. My mum left the hospital and left me with some chicken legs she had brought up for me, bless her, I ate them for the hospital food was disgusting. I had been in the hospital for a while, I can't remember how long, my memory is pretty vague during this period of time, but I know it was the same day that Mum had come up that the nurses took my blood pressure and told me it had gone down. Naturally I thought they would be sending me home, which I was not happy with. I was getting into my clothes and getting ready to go, the next minute I was surrounded by doctors, nurses, so many people, I remember the curtain being pulled round my bed. I recall someone mentioning that a paediatrician was on his way to talk to me. What the hell was going on here, it was chaos. I was approached by the paediatrician and was told that he is from the Special Care Baby Unit and that they was going to have to do an emergency caesarean and that my baby may not make it. They said if it does survive they will do everything in their power to save it. They asked me if I wanted to make a phone call, which I did, I spoke to my husband and told him what was happening. He turned round and said 'I can't bloody stop work now I have a living to make!' I walked back to the ward completely broken, my mind had collapsed. I was given a pre-med to make me feel drowsy and was wheeled down to the operating theatre. The anaesthetic kicked in, but I was not fully under when they made an incision in my stomach. I tried to put my head up to let them know I was awake, I could not move or speak for I was too weak and drowsy from the anaesthetic, eventually I must have passed out.

I awoke not knowing where I was or what was going on. My stomach was sore; I looked down to see there were large staples keeping my stomach together. I noticed I was alone, until a nurse came in with a Polaroid photo and told me I had a tiny daughter. She produced this picture, which looked like a little alien; all I could see were veins and bones lightly covered by a thin layer of skin. I felt nothing, my mind had gone into shock before they done the caesarean, as far as I was concerned my baby was dead. I screwed the photo up and threw it across the room. There still was no sign of my husband, but in walked his brother and my sister-in-law, my husband arrived ten minutes later.

Rob showed no emotion whatsoever, no words of comfort, not a cuddle, absolutely nothing. I was wheeled up to the Premature Baby Unit, I felt numb, incoherent, my eyes felt vacant. In an incubator with wires everywhere, laid my daughter, she was so tiny, she arrived two months premature and weighed two pounds four ounces. I looked at her and felt nothing. I had a full breakdown. I was told that my baby had not been feeding from me and that was the reason she was not growing. I had ballooned to eleven and a half stone, must have been the Guinness I was drinking when I was carrying her, I was told the iron was good for me, and as an alcoholic – I did not need to be told twice. I stayed in the hospital for ten days after she was born to enable me to try and bond with her. It was horrific, I could not breastfeed, though I did try, my daughter, who I named Sarah, was too tiny to latch on to me and was not responding. I would hold her little body and stare at her day after day but there was nothing there, it was hell seeing this tiny little thing, so fragile that I had brought into this world but could not love her.

I eventually left hospital with my daughter wrapped in my arms. I felt like I was going into the unknown and I was frightened. My husband thought it was a good idea to fit a new kitchen the day I came home with our baby. The flat looked like a bomb had dropped on it, there was debris everywhere. Whatever possessed him to re-fit a new kitchen the day our baby was coming home? I needed space and order to try and get things organised, but could not find space anywhere to do this, the place was blitzed.

As the weeks passed, I sank further away from reality, my depression went into psychosis and my thoughts and behaviour were disturbingly irrational. I felt claustrophobic and agoraphobic, I felt fearful of staying indoors on my own, and was attending to Sarah's needs systematically; I went into auto pilot. As my depression progressed, I stopped washing and cleaning my teeth; I would wear the same clothes for days on end. I would look in the mirror and not recognise the person staring back at me, I would look at my hands and think they did not belong to me, I knew I had lost the plot and was slipping into insanity but could not help myself. I cried every waking hour, I was not eating and hardly slept. My husband was no use to me whatsoever. He continued going out and getting drunk, with no thought of what was happening to me. I was in hell.

One morning, my mother knocked on the door. She was horrified and could not believe was she was seeing. I remember her gathering my belongings up and telling me I was coming with her. She grabbed my daughter and took us back to her house. She was mortified at the state I was in and called my health visitor who came to see me a few days later. I was diagnosed with severe psychotic depression by my doctor. My health visitor told Mum that she had never seen anyone whose depression was as severe as mine. Mum and my stepdad tried everything in their power to help me with Sarah. I could not eat, so mum would put a spoon of food in my mouth and feed me like a baby. She reminded me to wash and change my clothes every morning. I could not be left in a room on my own without freaking out. I was on various medications which I felt at the time was not helping at all, I even considered storing them up and when I had enough, take the lot. Suicide was the only way out, but the problem was I did not have the courage to carry this out. I took a few handfuls on one occasion, but something outside of my understanding stopped me, I believe looking back, in hindsight, it was God at work. I will elaborate on my relationship with him later on.

My illness was taking its toll on my mother and stepfather. My stepfather was mentally ill himself, he was diagnosed with Paranoid Schizophrenia and Mum was on the verge of a breakdown too. I could see what my illness was doing to them both, I felt so powerless and frustrated especially when I looked at my little girl whom I longed to love more than anything. I could not comprehend that how I could, as a mother, not feel the warmth, the joy, the unconditional love that I witnessed other mothers experience when they have a new born baby. The sheer and utter frustration and the torment filled the whole of my being when I saw other mothers holding their babies, bursting at the seams with joy and happiness. Why could I not feel how they felt? It even occurred to me that I must be evil and heartless, with no good inside me at all. Had the harsh realities of my past turned me into some kind of monster?

My husband made no effort to contact me or inquire about our daughter – he could not care less. This hurt me deeply, how anyone could be so callous and ruthless, is beyond my comprehension as a human being. My condition got so bad that I was referred to a psychiatrist at Hillingdon Hospital. I now believed that I was totally insane and would spend the rest of my life in a secure psychiatric unit. One morning, as I was changing Sarah's nappy, I had a vision of me swinging her round and round by her legs. I now thought I was going to harm my beautiful daughter, it was the most disturbing thought I could have ever encountered. I told my psychiatrist what happened and before long, I found myself in the car with Mum and my stepfather, heading off to Shenley, a psychiatric hospital that had a mother and baby unit. As I stepped out of the car, I was approached by a patient who had blood stains all down her skirt, she told me 'Don't come in here, you will never get out.' I was horrified, I could not be put away in there. Mum held my hand as we entered the building. We were greeted by a nurse who told us we would be seen to shortly. I wanted to die; the thought of being locked up in this hell hole with my daughter was too much for me to bear. I told the psychiatrist that his face did not look right, and that my hands were not mine. As alarming and crazy as it sounds, this was the state of my mind. He showed Mum and me to the room that I would be sleeping in, it really was my biggest nightmare come true, I really am crazy, it finally happened, everything I feared as a child was finally coming true. I clung hold of Mum's arm and begged her not to let them take me and my daughter. Mum was crying and told the psychiatrist that she would continue to look after me and my child. It's like she knew if I went in there, I would never come out, that made two of us. To my relief, Mum convinced the doctor that she could cope and home we went.

I don't know what I would ever have done, or what would have become of me, if it was not for my mother and stepfather. My mother and I may not have had the closest of relationships when I was growing up, and yes I did feel that she didn't love me as much as she loved my twin sister when I was younger, but her love really shone through when I needed her most. As for my stepfather and all that I put him through from the first moment I met him, I began to realise that he was not such a bad person after all, and the support he had given me through this horrific time in my life, would never be forgotten.

My daughter had been amazing throughout my illness from the time she came out of hospital. It was like she knew somehow that her Mum was very ill and slept right through the night, to let me rest. She was growing into such a beautiful child, she had big blue eyes and fine blonde hair. How could I not feel the love towards her that I so desperately wanted to, more than anything else in the world? It was torture. The longing for the love to fill my heart for her, tormented my every waking hour. One morning, my mother had to go out and do some shopping and have a much-needed break from me, she was going to the pub after for a drink. I still could not be left in a room on my own, but Mum was at breaking point by now and had to have some space. Being aware of this, I convinced her I would be okay, knowing deep down I was terrified but I had to let her go. She told me not to answer the phone for she feared that my husband might call, which could have an effect on me that could be lethal in my state of mind. Mum had only been gone ten minutes and I was freaking out, pacing the floor, terrified out of my mind then the phone rang. I was such in a state that I answered it, at least there would be a voice I can listen to down the phone. I recognised the voice on the other end, it was my husband. He asked me to meet him at the park which was about a ten minute walk away. I agreed and put the phone down. Shaking from head to toe, I realised that I would have to go out on my own which I have not been able to manage since I became ill. I put my daughter in her pram and opened the front door. Everything was spinning round, I felt paranoid and thought everyone in the street was looking at me, I thought I can't do this. An hour and a half later, I got to the entrance of the park and was greeted by my husband drunk out of his mind. He did not even notice his daughter in the pram next to me. He asked me if I had any money on me, which I did, I emptied my purse into the palm of his hands, I waited for that much needed cuddle and reassurance I so desperately longed for, but to no avail. The bastard put the money in his pocket and walked off, leaving me standing there beside my daughter's pram. Again, I had been rejected and this was the final nail in my coffin. I thought I could not feel any lower than I had been before I set off to meet him. I slipped further down into the black abyss that I was already in.

I have no memory of getting back to Mum's house, but I obviously did. By the time Mum got home, I was inconsolable, I told her what happened and she hit the bloody roof. She picked up the phone and went hell for leather at that heartless excuse for a man, I heard her say 'You have nearly put my daughter in a mental institution you bastard.' It's a good job he was not in the same room as her, for she would have killed him for what he had put me through.

A few months had passed since Mum rescued me from that monster of a husband. My daughter was now starting to grow and thrive and regardless of the fact that I still could not take care of myself, I could attend to my daughters every need (how I managed baffles me to this day). I truly believe the love was always there from the beginning of my daughter's life, but I was suffering the effects of my own childhood traumas, which I had suppressed since I found alcohol as it blocked my mind from feeling my emotions. My father passing away, then ending up with a heartless man who was emotionally constipated and made my life a living hell, finally pushed me over the edge. Looking back, with all that I had encountered from a very young age, it does not surprise me at all that I eventually completely broke down. The human mind can only take so much.

Chapter Eleven

The Miracle

I had never believed in miracles, but something happened one morning which was to be the happiest day of my life. I woke up very early this particular morning and cried as I always did the minute my eyes opened. I sat up and stared down to where my daughter was lying in her bed. I stretched my arms out to pick her up and held her close to my skin. I kissed her soft little forehead, then the miracle happened – I felt this overwhelming sense of warmth, love and devotion, a love so pure and unconditional, it was like holding a precious stone that goes beyond value. Every ounce of every emotion had been drawn to the surface of my being; the love that had been lying dormant within me was now present. I looked at my daughter who I had wanted to love and cherish and she looked up at me with eyes so bright and full of wonder. I realised, at this point, that I was not an evil person with no love in her heart and the truth of it was, that I was not responsible for the empty feelings and my poor state of mind. I had mentally broken down and was powerless over the feelings inside of me. I strongly feel that one of the reasons my daughter came in to this world was to save me. I have no reservations whatsoever, that if it had not been for my little miracle, I would not be here today to tell my story, which will become more clearer as you continue on my journey with me.

I had not touched alcohol since I became ill. This was not a conscious decision, I would imagine that I was so absorbed in my psychosis that the props I had used to hold me up and the coping defence mechanisms I had mastered to shield me from the harsh realities of my existence were not relevant, for I had lost perspective of my place in the world and who I was.

I cannot remember who took me, but I found myself sitting in a pub. I have no idea how this came to be considering I could not be left in a room alone. This had been the first time I left the house without being accompanied by my mother in many months; my memory is shot to pieces reflecting back at this period of time. I do recall getting rather drunk and experiencing that feeling of 'normality'. It felt like I had stepped back into my own body and the feeling of being outside of myself looking in had disappeared. The next morning another miracle happened, I woke up, no tears, nothing, my depression had vanished into thin air. This must sound a bit extreme, but it's true. I was informed by my health visitor that the medical profession thought that as my depression was one of the worst types they have experienced in their line of work, that they doubted very much that I would ever come out of it. It was a mystery to us all, but a very much welcomed one for me.

Not long after my miraculous recovery I realised that I did not want any connection with my husband whatsoever. I wanted him out of my life for good. One morning I decided to make an appointment to see a solicitor about starting divorce proceedings. They had arranged to see me that same day, I asked my brother Brady to come with me for moral support. I mentioned taking a restraining order out on my husband to keep him well away from my daughter and myself. The next day, I marched to the property that I still owned with my husband, put the key in the door and was greeted with Rob lying in a urine-soaked bed. He woke up and looked at me like he had seen a ghost, for I was the last person he thought would be standing there. Reverse psychology was something I could have a masters in; I asked him if he would like some breakfast and maybe a cup of tea followed by a nice cold can of lager. He was confused to say the least. Why would she be so nice to me after all I put her through? he must have thought to himself. Everything was going according to plan, he had his breakfast alright, right over his head, followed by a can of beer and a packet of pampers. Boy, was this a sight to have seen. As I walked out the front door I yelled 'You will be hearing from my solicitor,' – mission accomplished.

Within days my solicitor had rushed two restraining orders through the courts, one against me and the other against my daughter. A date was to be arranged for a court hearing in regards to the property that I desperately needed to move back into with Sarah and get this thug out. The day arrived for the hearing; my neighbour came with me to give me moral support. I waited patiently for my husband to turn up with his legal representative, but he never made it, fantastic, the hearing could not have gone better. It was ordered that his name would be taken off the property and the bailiffs would serve him the papers for him to leave the property giving him just a few hours to gather his things together. They asked me if I would like to go with them which I agreed I would. My husband answered the door shouting and swearing like a lunatic when they escorted him away. I stepped into my property and had the shock of my life. He had demolished everything in the flat: the walls of every room were slashed deep into the walls with a Stanley knife, the light fittings on the ceiling were pulled out with the wires exposed, which was highly dangerous and the bathroom had been smashed up. I could hardly believe what I was seeing. Every bit of furniture was shattered in to pieces. My daughter's cot and everything else that was hers had been destroyed, even the heads of all her teddy bears had been ripped off. As if this was not bad enough, I found letters stating the flat was up for repossession, he had not been paying the mortgage.

Sitting on the floor with my daughter, surrounded by debris, I did not know where to start. I had little money for food and God only knew how I was going to find the money to replace everything in the flat that that husband of mine had destroyed. I managed to gather a cot, clothes for my daughter and bits of furniture that people kindly gave to me. The building society empathised with my situation and were happy for only the interest to be paid on the mortgage for the time being giving me time to sort myself out.

Chapter Twelve

Venus Flytrap

Before long I returned back to the bottle and drank my worries away. This was something I always returned to when the going got tough. I did not know how to deal with my emotions but when putting alcohol into my system, I found that false sense of security and felt that I could handle anything. But when I was sober, my emotions were too overpowering to handle.

My mother would babysit for me which gave me some freedom to go out. Although I was a mother, I was still young and started partying again. I was back to my old behaviour of how I used to be before I met Rob. The only difference was that it was not just me now who I had to take care of – I had to be responsible now that I had a daughter to look after. As much as I wanted to be a good mother and give my daughter the emotional stability that I felt I never had as a child, I still craved and wanted the freedom to go out and do as I pleased.

I was well and truly damaged and screwed up to the max before my marriage and depression but now I had even more baggage to carry on my shoulders. Anger and resentment were eating away at me; every man was going to pay now for what my husband done to me. The drinking had progressed at a fast rate by now and I had to drink more to feel the effects because my tolerance was increasing. I endured emotional and mental torture each time I found myself waking up in unfamiliar beds with strangers I had picked up the night before. The guilt and shame of my behaviour was excruciating. I felt utter disgust and loathed myself. That I could disrespect my body the way I did when I was drunk made me physically sick. I had to have that morning drink to enable me to get up and function, to stop the tremors and the racing heart beat. The alcohol would relieve me of the mental torture I was in. After topping up my alcohol levels, the remorse would slowly disappear. As soon as I was back on my feet again, I would make my excuses and dash out the front door as fast as I could.

When I returned to pick my daughter up, I would say to myself, what kind of a mother am I behaving in this despicable manner? I knew, in my heart, that this behaviour was wrong, and my daughter deserved better. I should be putting all my energy into raising my daughter and staying out of the pubs and not putting myself about like some loose brazen hussy. Regardless of what my conscience was telling me, I struggled to change my behaviour. I continued to meet and date all types of men from different walks of life. I remember an American guy who was in the navy, a good looking man who had stability and was not short of a bob or two. I dated him for some time and enjoyed the lifestyle he gave me, buying me clothes, taking me to the finest restaurants and more importantly ,supplied me with as much Jack Daniels as I could possibly drink. This relationship eventually came to an abrupt end. Apparently unbeknown to me, he got down on one knee one night and asked me to marry him, naturally I said 'yes', I would tell men anything I thought they wanted to hear as long as I got what I wanted. He also informed me that night that he was being posted abroad and had a choice of countries where he could work. One being America and the other being Hawaii, I must have told him I fancied Hawaii for I had agreed to ship our belongings out there. When he came home from work the next evening full of the joys of spring and produced a lovely diamond engagement ring and told me he had informed his boss of where he would like to be posted, I gasped in shock horror. I had no recollection whatsoever of this arrangement the night before. I told him I was drunk and did not know what he was talking about and that I was not going anywhere. After a few harsh words were exchanged, off he went, brokenhearted. After I had managed to put the drink down for a while, the reality of what I had done to this poor innocent man whose only crime was to love and be with me, hit me like a bolt out of the blue. The self-hatred, the bewilderment at how I could have been so cruel and callous to an innocent, kind man was beyond belief. I isolated and withdrew myself from the outside world as much as I could. I was absorbed by the guilt and shame. It was like I was two different people with a split personality. When alcohol was in my system I became self-centred, selfish, unreliable, and unpredictable. My thinking became distorted and irrational; I seemed to live in the moment, without a thought or care for my behaviour and actions. I often wondered, in my sobering short-lived moments, why can't I allow someone, especially someone kind and genuine to love and take care of me, why did I feel the need to push them away when I had won their affections? Could it be that deep down I felt unworthy of being happy and loved? Did I feel that I needed to drink and get drunk to become more exciting and interesting because I feared they would not like me just for who I really was when sober? Was it also that I was drawn to emotionally unavailable men and destructive relationships because I felt less threatened by them and was therefore not so frightened of the possibility of them finding out who I really was – a rather shy sensitive person with numerous insecurities. On the other hand, I may have feared that men who were emotionally and mentally grounded, who were secure and self-reliant, would be more prone to seeing right through me and when I had been sussed, I would be abandoned by them. Maybe this is why my behaviour towards these types of men made me feel more insecure and the fear that they would leave me was much greater. I would sabotage the relationship because they would eventually leave me anyway, so I guess I got in there first to save them the job.

The American base was to be one of the places I hung out especially on Friday nights. The American men loved English women, which I used to my advantage. I met another American who was at least twenty years older than me and absolutely loaded. He had his own ranch in Canada and property in Rochester, New York. One night he took me, Mum and my stepfather out to a swinging jazz night. Mum's eyes lit up when he dropped down on one knee and proposed to me in front of everyone. Mum was kicking me under the table and nodding her head, she knew he was loaded and my daughter and I would live the life of Riley and not want for anything. Of course I said 'yes', what a knees-up we all had that night. The next morning was no laughing matter, for I woke up in his apartment – Mum had looked after my daughter all night, so me and this millionaire could get more acquainted. I reached out for the bottle of Jack that was not far from my bed and took the biggest gulp I possibly could, aaaah what have I gone and done now, why was I lying next to this overweight wrinkly yank who was old enough to be my grandfather? Yet again, those terrible feelings came back again, remorse, guilt and bewilderment, the memory of him asking me to marry him and saying yes mortified me. What was I going to do now? How could I possibly be so cruel? This man was kind and gentle, just like the other American, I felt sick knowing that I had led him on and was playing with his feelings. After a few more glasses of whisky, my conscience deserted me, the guilt and shame disappeared, just as it always did when I drank alcohol. We left his flat and I asked him to drop me at Mum's to pick up my daughter and said I would call. Mum was disappointed when I told her that I could not marry this man regardless of how much money he had, I just could not go through with it. Getting shot of him was not an easy task at all. He would leave roses outside my front door, he would be yelling crying and screaming through my letterbox, God it was awful. Eventually I found out that he had to have counselling to help him get over the hurt that I caused him by calling it off. Like many times before, when the alcohol was put down and reality struck, my heart went out to yet another victim that I had treated so appallingly. Living inside my head and always present were those terrible crippling feelings of self-hatred and remorse at what I had put this man through and how much he must have suffered. It made me just want to put alcohol in my system to make these feelings go away.

Life was one big piss-up for me, drinking my way through most days had become the norm – like it was years ago in my teenage years. I was seriously unhappy with most areas of my life; the only person that kept me going was my daughter. I befriended a Greek man who owned the restaurant below where I lived; he was an old man who worked every hour, day and night, running his business by himself. He was very kind to me and gave me a dining room table and chairs which he had in his restaurant. I would sit there drinking his booze and eating meals that I got for free, which again, I took advantage of. I asked him one day if I could borrow a thousand pounds for I wanted to take my daughter to America with Mum and Rob. My twin lived in New Orleans and my elder sister in Florida. I agreed that I would give him his money back when I sold my flat, which I had no intention of doing. He had a contract drawn up but I did not notice that it was to be paid back with interest. Crafty bastard got one over me. The four weeks in America was the worst holiday I have ever been on. I stayed for two weeks in New Orleans with my twin and her husband, who I did not like very much at all. He was a miserable old git moaning and giving his orders out, I was having none of it. I managed to get out in the evenings, but I found that babysitters were an expensive business; their fees were a lot higher than what they are in England. I got engaged in the little time I spent there, doing my usual stunt, promising men the world to get what I wanted, then came the inevitable, dumping them, the nasty person again surfaced when loaded with booze. My time in Florida was very short-lived, I must have stayed there a couple of nights when I found myself walking the streets of Florida at six o'clock in the morning, my daughter in my arms, with no idea where the Greyhound coach station was. The night before my sister had insisted that I go to this nightclub with her. We pulled two guys and took them back to her apartment. I ended up swimming and playing about in the sea whilst she was indoors getting pissed and was furious, because her companion had passed out leaving her sitting there with no one to drink with. She came flying out onto the beach, kicked the guys out, and told me to get out. She unplugged the phone so I could not even call a cab. I was drunk and soaking wet from the sea. I begged and pleaded for her to sleep on it until the morning, but there was no reasoning with her whatsoever. Fortunately, an old couple who were getting ready to open up their store approached me, I told them my situation and thankfully the old guy drove me to the coach station. That was the end of my holiday, bloody nightmare. I did not speak to my sister for years after that, I believe alcohol yet again was doing its worst.

When I returned to England, the Greek guy and I fell out and he took me to court over the money I owed him, I represented myself which did not go down too well for I was pissed as usual and got laughed out of court, ending up with a caution slapped on my property. Yet again, I found myself all alone and struggling to get by on ten pounds a week, which was all I had left after paying the bills. It was to be my daughter's first Christmas; it was a depressing time of the year for me, having hardly any money and no plans for the festive season. Mum was going away to Butlin's holiday camp, and it was looking like I would be spending Christmas alone with my daughter. I managed to borrow enough money to get my daughter some presents and some food for us and resigned myself to the fact that this Christmas was going to be a lonely one, until I met a man the day before Christmas Eve. He was working as a builder at Sainsbury's which was just round the corner from where I lived. He chatted me up in my local pub one dinner-time and, before the day was out, we became an item. How lovely I thought, the timing could not have been better with Christmas just round the corner, maybe I won't be lonely after all. The same night I invited him round for a drink, he arrived later on that evening with a couple of bottles of my favourite Jack Daniels. The night was going well until an old boyfriend turned up at my door, which eventually turned into a brawl, my new boyfriend turned out to be extremely possessive even though I had just met him, he thought he owned me, my ex-boyfriend left, and the rest of the evening was spent arguing until I passed out. The next morning was Christmas Eve; I had left my new boyfriend asleep on the couch the night before. When I got up there was no sign of him. As I looked around the living room, I noticed all the presents, even the ones for my daughter, had disappeared, so had my purse with the little money I had left to last me over the Christmas period. That wicked swine had robbed me, I was in bits, how could anyone do that? To take a child's Christmas presents was the lowest of the low! I sobbed my heart out and called Mum to come over, Mum had her suspicions about him, for she was in the pub the day that I first met him. My mother, I have to be honest, always seemed to be there for me when I was in trouble. She had turned out to be a very caring person, I really was coming round to the fact that my mother did love and care for me after all. I did have resentment towards her, for I always blamed her for the break-up of her marriage with my father. As I was growing older myself, I realised that Dad had his faults too. Mum eventually went and I wondered what I was going to do now. Thankfully there were a few presents that I had not wrapped yet in my wardrobe for my daughter, at least she had a few to open on Christmas day. The day passed slowly and I could not wait for it to be over. I put my daughter to bed that evening and fell asleep on the couch. I am so grateful that my daughter was not old enough to understand what was going on, and that she was spared all this upheaval I was going through. I was woken in the early hours of the morning by a figure leaning over me in the dark with his hand round my mouth. It was the bastard who robbed me; he had smashed my bedroom window and crept in when I was sleeping on the couch in the living room. This man was trying to strangle me, I could feel his hands squeezing my neck as tight as he could, I could hardly breathe; he was killing me. I don't know where I got the strength from but somehow I managed to push him off me. He fell backwards into a wall unit that came down on top of him, which gave me time to grab my daughter and get out of the flat. He managed to get away by the time the police arrived. Shocked and shaken I gave my statement to the police. I feared that he would be back to finish me off. I feared for the safety of my daughter, I did not want to stay in my flat but had nowhere else to go. I slept with a metal bar by my side in case this monster returned. Months later I got a visit from the police, they informed me that they had caught the man who assaulted me. Apparently he had been on the run and had escaped from prison, he was a con artist and it was not the first time he had assaulted women. He had a long history of the same behaviour he inflicted on me and was sent back to prison for a very long time.

My daughter had blossomed into a beautiful one-year-old; she was adorable and I was so blessed to have her, some days I often wondered if I was dreaming all of this, she made my life worth living and gave me everything to live for. I had not heard anything from her father, not a birthday or Christmas card, he disowned her and in a way I am glad of his lack of involvement in her life, considering the person that he was. I was still struggling to make ends meet financially, going shopping was a depressing time for me. I would watch other mothers pushing their trolleys loaded up with food I could not afford. I would hide my tears behind my sunglasses which I wore from the time I got up in the morning, to hide my sadness from the world around me. I would try to entertain my daughter by teaching her to sing and dance as she got a bit older. She would copy me when I would do aerobics in my living room, for I could not afford to go to classes. Our weekends were spent down the local park, she would let me push her on the swings all day long, and like most children, would cry when it was time to go home. I spent a lot of time gazing out of my windows observing other people who seemed so happy and carefree, I would look at couples walking by hand in hand, staring in to each other's eyes with love in their hearts, oh I wished I could find someone to love and share my life with.

Chapter Thirteen

Not Very Vice

At this point in my story, I am wondering whether I should tell the truth about the next episode of my life and risk being judged and ridiculed. After giving this a lot of thought, I realised that my book would not be complete if I left it out. It is crucial that I am rigorously honest in every area of my experience to enable people who are reading this to get a clear and precise picture of who I really am and where I have come from. Of course, I am leaving myself wide open to criticism, but this is a risk I am willing to take.

One morning I was flicking through the local newspaper, trying to find some kind of work where I could get paid cash in hand; I could not go on living on the bread line. I was sick of the hand-me-down clothes I dressed my daughter in and was fed up with scrambled eggs and beans on toast for my dinner. I came across an advertisement for working as an escort. To be honest I was not sure what an escort did, so I dialled the number. A Chinese woman answered the call; she asked me if I had experience, which naturally I said I did. She mentioned something about an agency fee I would have to pay out of my earnings, which I agreed to. She asked when I was available and said she would get back to me. Later on that day she called and told me I would start work the next morning. She gave me a phone number to call to arrange to meet my client and hung up. I called the number and a very charming man answered, he asked me what I looked like, what my measurements were. Was he going to buy me something to wear? I did not have a clue what the hell this was all about. He said he would meet me at nine thirty the next morning outside the station.

My alarm went off at seven. I got up and dropped my daughter at my mum's. I told her I had found a job and would explain later when I picked my daughter up. I was so nervous; I knocked back three quarters of a bottle of vodka which I got from the supermarket downstairs. I had no money left for food now. I was flat broke. I had no idea what to wear, I imagined I would be escorting this man to a business lunch or maybe he just wanted someone to talk to, so I put on a smart skirt and blouse and headed off to the station, still baffled as to what was expected of me. I nervously waited for this man to appear, I was paranoid that people were looking at me, for I was slightly pickled from the vodka. My gut feeling told me something dodgy was going on, but I could not put my finger on it until a Mercedes pulled up with tinted windows, there sat a big black man, he looked at me and asked if I was Gina. I was told to change my name when I was inquiring about the job; I thought this rather odd. Why did I have to change my name? It sounded a bit daft to me. I took one look at him turned on my heels and headed off in the other direction. I don't know why I reacted like this; it must have been my gut feeling trying to tell me something again. The guy followed me down the road and asked me not to be scared and get in the car. Well, I got in this big flash car that had a minibar in the back, he told me to help myself and I did not need telling twice. After a few glasses of brandy were swiftly poured down my throat, my fear had been replaced by excitement. Ooh, look at me I thought, feeling like a V.I.P. being carted off to a secret destination, maybe a flash restaurant in London, or maybe the theatre to see a show, the anticipation was growing at the same rate as the brandy I was chucking down my throat.

After travelling for about half an hour, he pulled up outside a huge house which was being renovated, there were builders everywhere. Maybe he had to pick something up, no problem I thought, I had my minibar in the back, he could take as long as he liked. The door was opened for me, I was told to get out and follow him. Not so amused now, I was wondering what on earth was going on here. I found myself entering a bedroom with nothing but a bed in. He poured me a large glass of wine, told me to relax and take my clothes off. You cheeky devil I thought and slapped him round the face, what did he think I was, some kind of hooker? Yes, that's exactly what he thought. He told me it was obvious it was my first time and there was nothing to worry about. What happened to the slap-up meal, theatre, I was naively mortified until a big wad of fifty pound notes appeared in his hand; I had never seen this amount of money before in my life. The thought of all the money I owed the building society and the little amount I was merely surviving on made me question whether it would be so bad, considering the fact I was rather promiscuous, at least I would not be giving it away for free. A good few glasses of wine, combined with the three quarters of vodka I had before I left my flat that morning and the amount of brandy I had put away on the journey here, were starting to take its toll. Before I had time to make a decision, the dreaded deed was done and dusted. As I gathered my clothes from the floor and began to dress, I felt very uncomfortable, but relieved at the same time. I kidded myself I was fine with what just had occurred, but really I felt cheap, dirty and rather disgusted with myself. I tried to rationalise it in my head and tried to make myself feel better by thinking, at least I wasn't hanging out on street corners swinging my handbag and chewing gum like proper hookers do, I was better than that, wasn't I? None of the justifications I could think of to make me feel better worked. I began to think about my daughter, what kind of a mother does this? How was I going to feel later on down the line when she gets older? What would she think of me? Would she believe me when I told her that I done this for her so we could keep a roof over our heads and not worry about where the next meal was coming from? Would she blame herself for putting me through this? All these questions were spinning around in my head, I needed more alcohol to cloud over these feelings which I could not handle.

With a big bundle full of fifties, I headed back to the station where I was picked up and made my way towards my local pub feeling like I had just won the lottery on one hand, but on the other, I felt dreadful. I turned a few heads when I hung onto the bar for dear life, for my legs struggled to hold me up. I offered to buy everyone in the pub a drink and boy did I become popular all of a sudden. I must have passed out soon after going back to the flat, for I was woken by my phone ringing, it was the Chinese lady who ran the escort agency wondering how I got on this morning. She asked me if I was available for work that evening and gave me another number to call. I felt like death, the drinking session had done me in. After a few liveners of vodka I was pickled again and off on my way to meet my client. My stomach was churning and I felt sick, I knew what I was doing was so wrong, but I just focused on the money and kept thinking I would be out of debt before long then all this would come to an end. My client took me to a large house out in the country which was very secluded; I sensed this was not a good idea, for there were no other houses around. A few more drinks and the fear subsided as usual. Unusually, the fear returned not long after. I closed my eyes and just wanted this to be over. After it was all over, I realised I had not received the money up front. When I politely asked my client for my fees, he pulled a knife from out of the drawer and threatened to kill me. I was terrified and ran out the front door as fast as my legs could carry me – he could have killed me. I did not mention this to my boss, for I was worried that if I did he would hunt me down. I started to question whether this was worth risking my life for, my daughter could end up without a mother, I was confused and my thoughts were all over the place. I was aware that I had to consume larger amounts of alcohol to get me through this. If I was sober, never in a million years would I or could I ever have put myself through such an ordeal – not a chance in hell.

I had to re-evaluate my situation but the greed and hunger for money overpowered my instincts and I continued to progress in this seedy life of vice. I worked every waking hour I could, some days I would easily earn a thousand pounds. This was all well and good as I counted my stash every night, but the drinking, smoking marijuana and the lack of sleep was having a terrible effect on me psychologically and physically; I was burning out. Did I feel guilty and shameful the way I was living my life? At this stage, no, I don't think I did. I had convinced my troubled mind that it was okay and I was not hurting anyone else except for myself. In a sick kind of way it suited me, not just from a financial aspect, but it also gave me a feeling of control. I hated men and, as I mentioned earlier, I was going to make every man pay, now in more ways than one, for the damage and torment my ex-husband had put me through and the fundamental abuse I had suffered at the hands of many men. I felt superior in a twisted kind of way, when the money was exchanged I inwardly thought, you sad bastards, having to pay a woman for sexual pleasures, there was only one winner here, and that was me. Through lack of self-awareness, I was ignorant to the fact that damage was being done. On top of the other baggage I had carried around with me since I was little, I was an absolute mess. My daughter was getting older now and I was thinking about how much longer I could keep this hidden from her, regardless of the fact she thought Mummy was at work, I felt my heart sink when I looked into her innocent looking eyes – what she would think of me, kept going round and round in my mind.

I met men from all walks of life, young, old, married men who claimed 'my wife does not understand me,' – that old chestnut. I did feel sorry for the wives who had no idea what was occurring behind their backs. I was not ruthless and deep down I was deeply sad and unhappy with my life and what I was doing with it. I had been working for a few years and, inevitably, had to tell Mum what I was doing for a living. She was not startled by my revelation but when I helped her out with a few quid for looking after my daughter, she did not want to accept, but I insisted. I am so grateful that my daughter was not at an age to question what was going on. There was no way that I was going to end up losing our home and living in a bed and breakfast. I wanted my daughter to have a nice home and to be in a position that she would not have to go without. More importantly, my daughter knew how much she was loved; she had security, stability, self-esteem and self-worth. Even if we ended up in a squat, she would have the nurturing, acceptance and encouragement that I believe every child needs to enable them to grow up to live a full and productive life. I was the end result of the lack of these vital ingredients and made damn sure I would give my daughter what I lacked as a child. But how did I manage to keep my sanity and be there emotionally for my daughter when I was an emotional wreck myself? Somehow, I managed to try and detach and separate myself from this destructive behaviour when I was working. It was like living two separate lives, being two different people.

I managed to pay all the arrears of my mortgage and replaced all the damage that my ex had done when we moved back in the flat. I had dated many men that I met through the agency, though it was not encouraged to get emotionally involved. I had holidays abroad which I ruined through my wild and reckless behaviour. I was, on many occasions, given the choice to stop working by clients who wanted to 'save me' from this destructive behaviour. As much as I wanted to be saved deep down, it was more important for me at this stage to be financially independent and stand on my own two feet, regardless of what this lifestyle was doing to me.

As my destructive life of vice continued, every part of me was breaking down physically and mentally, again, I felt that there was only so much the human body and mind could take. I was missing out on these vital important moments that I would never be able to get back with my daughter as she was growing up. I needed to spend more time being a mother and do all the things I should be doing, like tucking her in bed at night, reading her a bedtime story. Sooner than I anticipated, I decided to take a client of mine up on his offer to be supported by him and leave the seedy life of vice behind. I know I said I did not want to depend on a man to support me, but I guess I looked at the pros and cons of stopping working, and thought I would rather be financially looked after and spend more time with my daughter. I also needed rest and to let my mind and body heal, for it had been abused for so long.

This man was a Muslim who was devoted to his religion. I found out he had a wife and children, which I was not too happy about, but he would spend as much time as he could to be with me and my daughter. He paid the bills and groceries and as far as he was concerned, I was his woman. He had cast-iron rules – one being I was not allowed out in a pub for it was not the thing to do, he thought women should stay at home.

Turning my back on my life as an escort was a huge relief for me; it was soul-destroying and degrading. Whilst I was working I was not really in touch with the extent of the damage (physically, mentally and emotionally) caused by the abuse I endured during these years. Life was not a bed of roses now either, having to depend on my boyfriend to support me financially. He was a control-freak living a double life which I was not happy with – not just for mine and my daughter's sake, it was not fair on his wife and children either. The time came where I'd had enough of being controlled, bullied and not being able to go out and socialise, this was not what I imagined it to be. As I rebelled, the arguments would start, they were horrific, and I began to notice that this man was extremely selective with his religion. Having sex outside of his marriage with an escort, I would imagine would not be welcomed. I was torn between putting up with this nasty man or returning back to the life of vice, neither of which I wanted.

One day, I decided to go to the pub and meet up with Mum and some friends and thought to hell with him and his so called rules. After an afternoon of some very heavy drinking, through the pub doors he came and frogmarched me back to my flat. What happened when my front door was closed will remain with me forever. I was stripped naked and abused physically and sexually in every way imaginable. I was beaten up so badly that my ribs were bruised beyond recognition. My mouth was all over my face where he had hit me. He kept me prisoner inside the walls of my bedroom for four days. I had to use the floor as my toilet as he would not let me use the bathroom. It was disgusting, the humiliation of it all was soul-destroying. It crossed my mind throughout this ordeal that this was how my life was going to end, naked with a few ten pound notes surrounding my corpse. What a horrible way to die, and how startling it would have been for anyone who had found me. It crossed my mind that maybe I had brought this on myself, I was being punished for my behaviour and for all the men I had taken hostage, taken my rage and resentment out on, because of the hurt and pain I had suffered all my life.

My nightmare eventually came to an end when he had to go back and answer to his wife and children about where he had been all this time. During this ordeal, unbeknown to me, my mum had somehow managed to get his home telephone number. I imagine he must have called me from his home when I was at Mum's and his number was obviously not withheld. Mum being the shrewd woman that she was, wrote it down just in case, she knew he was married and did not like him at all. After a skinful she phoned him to give him a piece of her mind. But it was his wife who answered the phone. Mum told her everything, good old Mum. After receiving this devastating news, his wife fled the family home and got the first flight back to India. I really felt for that poor woman, yes, I was just as guilty as him, but I guess at least she was free from this vile man who must have given her a hell of a life, judging how he treated me. I eventually found out that he also fled the country, and had lost his business, his marriage and was living a life in squalor in Karachi. Thank God that my daughter was with her Nan for a few days, I could not imagine the effect it would have had on her to have witnessed the abuse that was inflicted on her mother whom she cherished.

The emotional and mental scars and the humiliation reduced me, at my lowest level, to self-harm, for the pain was overbearing. I slashed my face with a razor blade and ended up in a refuge for battered women. I had become a danger to myself. The embarrassment and excruciating shame I suffered for months whilst waiting for my face to heal was terrible. I isolated myself most of the time and only went out for fresh air after darkness fell. My confidence was at an all-time low, my counsellor at a women's centre thought it would be beneficial for me to attend a self-defence course. Holding my own was not a problem for me, my father taught me how to defend myself at a tender age, but the course offered me techniques designed to defend myself if I found myself in a similar situation to those which I had been in many times before.

Chapter Fourteen

Best Friend Turned Enemy

My face eventually healed but the emotional scars from all I had encountered since I was little remained inside of me and were really getting in the way and preventing me from living a full, happy and productive life. I was slowly committing suicide and drinking myself to death. I had no one to turn to and could not see a light at the end of this dark abyss that I was trapped in. I did not know what was happening to me, I searched and searched flicking through the pages of every self-help book I could get my hands on, seeking the answers to so many questions that were running through my mind. Nursing yet another mini nervous break-down, which most people would call a hangover, I found myself looking through a phone book and found a helpline for people who have problems with alcohol. I dialled the number and cried like a baby, I begged them to help me. They told me they would get someone to call me back; I waited anxiously for the phone to ring with a drink in my hand. I remember putting the phone to my ear and listening to a lady who started to tell me a little of her experience with alcohol, the identification was astounding, for the first time in my life I didn't feel alone. She arranged to pick me up the next evening and told me we were going to an AA meeting. All sorts of things were running through my mind, did I really want to be sitting amongst tramps who smelled swigging from a cheap wine bottle with urine stains down their trousers, I didn't think so, but by a twist of fate, I decided to go and take a look anyhow.

The next evening came round pretty quick; I decided I would not drink that day, which I seemed to manage, courtesy of a handful of Valium. This lady appeared at the door, not what I imagined at all; she was smartly dressed, looked respectable and did not stink of booze. She drove me to the meeting and suggested I just sit and listen, to try and look for the similarities not the differences.

I walked through the door like a terrified kitten, head facing the floor, my normal position. I sat at the back and looked around, I couldn't see any tramps or weirdos, just ordinary people who all appeared to be happy and joyous, I did not understand. What am I doing here, these people didn't have a problem with alcohol, they couldn't have, because if they did, they certainly would not be laughing, that's for sure. I could not believe what I was hearing; everything I heard, felt like they were talking about me. It was amazing, I had this feeling like I had just come home. So many questions that I had been searching for the answers to all of my life, were right here in that room. I discovered that I suffered from a killer disease called alcoholism; I learned that the illness is progressive, that it gets worse, never better. I also learned that I could live a happy and fulfilled life, one day at a time; I had a twelve-step programme that provided me with tools to help me deal with problems that occur in everyday life. The programme would help me become aware of my defects of character, which I was not aware of before I came to AA. Through applying these steps in my everyday life, my attitude would change, I would see life through a different set of glasses, not the rose-tinted ones that I had been wearing since the first time I put alcohol into my system.

Since that first meeting, I had hopes for the future, I had people who understood me and I began to realise that I was not going crazy – what a relief that was. I took to AA like a duck to water, a whole new world had opened up for me, and I felt alive for the first time in my life. I had people in my life who accepted me for who I was. Over the next few years my life changed so much, I began to discover who I really was. My ego was smashed to pieces, I came to realise that I was not the centre of the universe after all. What did knock me sideways was that everything I thought I was, I wasn't – what a smack in the guts was that. I learned how to be honest, firstly to myself and then to others. This was a huge turnaround for someone like me, who spent their whole life lying to everyone about everything. This revelation mortified me. When the pieces of the jigsaw started to form a clear picture of who I really was, I could see that I had allowed people to hold my happiness in their hands all my life, and that peace of mind had to come from within. The big one for me was that I had to learn to say 'no'. I was a *people-pleaser*, with hidden agendas that I was not even aware of. I came to trust in my own judgements and make decisions for myself.

Looking back to when I first took that drink of whisky from Mum's bottle, I now realised, from what I was beginning to learn about the disease of alcoholism, that I was allergic to alcohol. For why else would I have continued to drink considering how much I hated it and what it had done to my parents? I also discovered that once alcohol enters my system, it triggers of a compulsion to carry on and that I have no mental defence against. I believe that this illness mentally convinces you that you have not got it, for when the thought of having a drink enters my mind, my mind will try to convince me that it will be different this time. I think I will be able to drink like some other people I know do, my head will tell me I will be able to stop abruptly if I choose to, that I won't wake up in strange places with strange people I have never met before. I think that this time around I won't be pacing the floor shaking, panicking and turning my house upside down looking for a can or a bottle that I hid and forgot about. I can't control the thought of having a drink, but from my experience I know that I am responsible for what I do with the thought when it enters my mind and if I hold on to that thought long enough, I will inevitably drink to overcome the mental obsession. I would imagine that people who do not have an allergy to alcohol would question why someone would drink when they know what the consequences will be. The problem was, when I reflected on all the times I relapsed and all the insanity that went with it, I could remember what it was like very clearly, but I could not relive the feelings, the remorse, self-loathing, guilt and shame, terror and bewilderment . . . the list goes on. If I could remember how I felt back then, for just five minutes, the chances of myself picking up a drink again would be very slim.

After abstaining from alcohol for some time, I learned how to drive. After many driving lessons, I decided to put in for my test. Come the morning of my driving test, I found myself still paralytic from the drinking session the night before. I had half an hour's driving lesson before hand, which was disastrous, everything that could go wrong did. How I managed to swing this I do not know, surely it would have been obvious that I was acting strangely. Mind you, I could hold my drink at this stage of my drinking career and could function pretty well regardless of the quantity I could put away. When I reached the test centre, my nerves started to kick in, so much so that after meeting the examiner – who was a man, handy I thought – I got in the car and pulled away, forgetting about him and leaving him standing there on the kerb. Bloody hilarious, as I reversed back to pick him up, he could not help but laugh, which again was handy as it kind of broke the ice. The test only lasted fifteen minutes and I sailed through. I do not think that would have been the case if I was sober, thinking about it, I have never done anything important without having to put enough alcohol in my system to give me the courage I needed. I was greeted by my driving instructor who was waiting with anticipation to see how well or badly I had done. I was so excited that I had passed, for I had never passed anything in my life, except passing out. I wound the window halfway down and pulled him towards me to hug him, but his head got stuck in the window. The perfect ending to a perfect day.

Unfortunately, complacency set in, I thought I had cracked my alcoholism and picked up a drink again. Over the next few years I was in and out of AA, for there were some parts of me that I was still holding on to and did not want to let go of, and until I decided to let go of the corner of the towel I was hanging onto, I would not have continuous recovery. My drinking progressed like I was told it would, I found myself waking up lying in a pool of vomit in a gutter by the side of the road on the other side of London, not knowing how I got there. I was locked up in police cells, and suffered alcoholic poisoning on numerous occasions, it was hell. Money was tight and being tanked up and reckless, it was not long before I ended up working at the escort agency yet again. The torment I was in was hell on earth, for I remember hearing people saying at my first meeting, that a head full of AA and a belly full of beer does not go well together, oh, how right they were. Working for the agency this time around was worse than ever before, I hated it with a vengeance. The sleaziness, everything surrounding me made me feel physically sick. Mum started to become concerned, for I was looking ill and exhausted. She picked me up one day and pushed me into the back of the car and drove me to her mobile home near the sea. Whilst there my boss kept calling me to work and informed me that there was a client who was desperate to see me, he would not stop calling. When I returned, I agreed to see him. He was a young man who, for some reason, was different to the other strange weird and twisted men I had seen before. He was kind and gentle, he told me he had a feeling that would not leave him, and he had to see me. I believe this man was meant to come into my life to save me from this destructive dangerous game I was playing. He asked if he could spend all night with me and basically never left.

I stopped working and thought I had found love at long last. In the beginning I was the happiest woman alive, my daughter took to him straight away, I knew she could sense he was a good, decent and genuine man and did not feel the need to protect me, which she had done in the past. Life was pretty good – we enjoyed holidays together, my daughter was thriving at school and everything seemed perfect. Mal, was a happy-go-lucky person, he had been married twice before and both wives had done the dirty on him and left him for someone else. Considering the heartache he went through, he did not seem to hold grudges or harbour any resentments towards them. He was a very forgiving person. Not a day went by without him asking me to marry him, anyone would have been a fool not to, he was perfect, had no obvious addictions and carried very little baggage from his past. Men like him were very few and far between.

I don't know what happened or how this came about but out of the blue, I woke one morning with my partner lying next to me and as he turned to hug and kiss me good morning, I looked at him and shuddered, I could not bear for him to touch me. Up until that morning everything was great, I loved him making love to me, being around him made me happy, how could my feelings change so dramatically overnight? I could understand if he had shown a different side to him. But no, he was the same person that morning that he had been since the day I met him. I was so upset and confused, wondering what was wrong with me, and why I couldn't just be happy and sustain a healthy and wholesome relationship. The obvious was right there in front of me, but I was too damaged and shut-down to see it. I had no awareness of what I was thinking most of the time, due to anaesthetising any emotion, good or bad, that surfaced with alcohol and mind-altering chemicals. My life became one big lie again, now I was drinking and the suffering was endless.

During the next five years I made this lovely, genuine man's life a living hell. I would tell him I was just going to the shops and return three days later; I would be out drinking, taking drugs and being unfaithful. I would lie in bed for days unable to function, due to acute alcoholic withdrawals. Mal would have to take time off work to look after me and risk losing his job. I would deprive him of sex for months on end, leaving him feeling undesirable and rejected. I even got pregnant with someone else's child and made him pay for me to go to a private clinic for a termination. When I was not drinking, I hated myself for how cruel I was to him. I would swear that I would not go out days on end drinking again. I promised I would change and it would be different this time around. The reality of my behaviour, especially towards someone who had done everything for me and my daughter, was appalling. Drink turned me into a monster. I was not responsible for my actions when alcohol was in my system but afterwards, guilt and shame absorbed me. I would be inconsolable when I had sobered up and realised what I had been doing to him, it was like the devil had entered my soul and wanted me to sabotage everything good in my life. Mal deserved the love, affection, respect and acceptance, which I believe each and every one of us craves, for this priceless act of unconditional love. Before long, I found myself going out alone, propping up the bar, taking drinks from strangers I had just met and sometimes I would find myself coming to in a strange bed with someone I did not know. It was like the self-destruct button was being pushed yet again, resulting in agonising guilt, shame and bewilderment. The look on Mal's face when I staggered through the door with bites on my neck, reeking of booze, still high as a kite from whatever drug I was taking the night before, killed me. I hated myself, again the endless broken promises 'never to do it again' were wearing thin now. Mal was on the brink of losing his job, for he could not go to work and leave my daughter in the early hours of the morning when I did not return home. Regardless of how badly I treated him and what I put him through, I was still treated like a princess, he would tuck me into bed and cook me breakfast, with no talk of my disappearance the night before.

I had ended up in accident and emergency on many occasions due to alcoholic poisoning, bad hallucinations or a bad reaction to the amount of drugs I would take when I was out on a mission. I went to see a specialist at the hospital, who told me that if I did not stop drinking I would be dead in the next couple of years. This was a wake-up call which did not last very long. Within a week, I was back out there, my drinking was completely out of control, my binges would sometimes last six months, sometimes a year or two, once I had that first drink, I could not stop. One morning I went to step out of bed after a heavy drinking session the night before, as I went to put my foot down, I fell straight to the floor. I had no feeling or sensation all the way down the left side of my body, I thought I'd had a stroke. I was terrified, my body and mind was breaking down but I could not stop myself from taking that first drink. I did eventually get the feeling back, which again was forgotten in no time at all. For ten years I had been taking Valium that I would get from a friend I knew, her doctor would hand them out like Smarties, – they don't do that nowadays. These prescribed drugs, unbeknown to me, were highly addictive. I would take them by the handful when I was withdrawing from alcohol, they settled my heart rate down and calmed the muscle tremors and the uncontrollable shakes. I was seriously addicted to them but did not realise this at the time.

Things had gotten so bad, that everyday life was an uphill struggle, especially looking after my daughter and trying to hide my addictions and the consequences from her. Very rarely would I openly drink in front of Sarah, but under no circumstances would I ever take drugs in her presence. She hated me drinking, she witnessed the depression and suffering I endured in the aftermath of every drinking session I had. I would look at her and see the fear and powerlessness in her eyes, it was heartbreaking, and it was like looking at me when I was a young girl. Even though her childhood was not traumatic like mine, it still had an effect on her, naturally.

The time eventually came where I could no longer put my partner through any more suffering, I had to set him free so he could have a chance of finding someone who could love and accept him for who he was. It broke my heart and his. Sarah was heartbroken, she was too young to understand why I had to do this. This must have been the first unselfish act I had ever done in my life, to put someone else's happiness before mine. Mal moved out and continued to pay the mortgage and bills for a while, which he really did not have to do, but that was the kind of person he was. I would have given anything to have had the capability to have been able to give and receive love, I just did not know how, for I was never shown.

Mal, as I mentioned before, paid my mortgage and bills after we parted, eventually this came to an end when he found someone else to love. This woman was controlling and manipulative, she dominated Mal and wanted him to break all ties with every involvement he had with me, including Sarah. This was devastating for her, Mal was the only father-figure she had ever known, it broke my heart and hers when Mal stopped all contact. I did not blame him for this, this was orchestrated by his partner, and for fear of losing her, he went along with it, regardless of how hurt he must have felt. Panic set in, how was I going to survive financially? There was no way on earth was I going to return to the seedy degrading life working for the agency. Fortunately, Mal let me have the use of the car, which enabled me to seek work doing contract cleaning. I had many cleaning jobs; I started work at six-thirty in the morning cleaning offices, and then went on to clean in people's private homes till early evening. Even though the money was poor, anything was better than what I used to do, I felt good about myself making an honest respectable living. Something happened one day when I was working for a schoolteacher who had two twin boys. One morning she told me that she would not be long, she was nipping out to take her boys to play group. As I was alone in the house, I thought I would have a bit of a nose round. I was pretty envious of all the material things this woman had. As I had been lost in thought, I hadn't realised time was moving on and it suddenly dawned on me that I had not done much work. I was asked to get the mini Hoover out to clean the boys' mattresses. As I was going about my business I found myself becoming aroused by the vibration of the Hoover being pressed against my crotch. Things got pretty intense so I proceeded to remove my jeans and underwear and fully indulge in this experience. As I was just about to climax, I noticed a pair of shoes standing there at the bottom of my feet. As I slowly moved my eyes upwards, I noticed there were legs in those shoes. It was the most embarrassing moment of my entire life; the women had arrived home and stood there looking at me in absolute horror. I was caught right on the spot, she screamed, I screamed, there was nothing I could do to get out of this – pardon the pun –sticky situation. The woman ran down the stairs calling me a pervert and said she was going to call the police. I got dressed and ran as fast as I could down the stairs and out through the front door. What was I to tell my boss when the police arrive at the office? Would I get done for indecent exposure, my God, what a bloody predicament I found myself in. Even though it was pay day, I cut my losses and left the company. I never did hear from the police thank God. That day I will never forget, mind you, I very much doubt she will either.

★★★

I did not go back to working for the escort agency, I was done with that way of life; it had beaten me into the ground. My behaviour still remained the same, men came in and out of my life, the drinking continued, but this time it was harder, for I did not have my partner to take care of me anymore. I was terrified of being alone, especially after the drink wore off. I thought, on many occasions, that I would be found dead on my own in my bed, the fear of dying tormented my every waking hour, I wanted to live, I worshipped my daughter and the thought of leaving her alone in this world was too much to bear. I had to get help before it was too late, I had to swallow my pride and make that phone call to a friend in AA, and this was my only chance. Although I did go back to my meetings, I struggled to stay sober for long periods of time; the more I slipped off the wagon the harder it was to get back on it again, I would walk back through the doors of AA with my tail between my legs. I made an appointment to see a doctor at the alcohol and drug clinic, for I could not cope with the horrific withdrawals, and I could not hold out long enough for them to pass, resulting in me having to take a drink to stop the panic attacks and the delirium tremens. The doctor prescribed me a drug which knocked out the withdrawals and gave me a chance to enter recovery again. I also discovered that I was a relationship addict, I had to have a man in my life to validate my existence, without a man, I did not feel alive, I was addicted to the drama and upheaval that exists in an unhealthy dysfunctional relationship. This is why my relationship with Mal did not work out, there wasn't any of the drama from his side of the relationship, the drama came from my behaviour when I drank. I could not handle a sensible and emotionally gathered man, who loved and respected me for who I was. For me, this was boring. I could not handle *nice*, for I had never had it. If I did not get the appropriate help for this self-destructive addiction I had in relationships, then my chances of recovery were very slim, for each time I got into a relationship I would sabotage it. As I mentioned before, I think, deep down, I felt like I was unlovable, I did not deserve to be treated nicely and had to drink when I got emotionally involved with someone for I felt I was not exciting enough, not good enough and did not have the confidence or the self-assurance to be who I really was. I never would allow myself to stick around long enough with somebody loving and caring to experience the feeling of being loved and accepted for who I really was. Through my relationships, I was searching, for something to fill this hole up I had inside of me that I could not fill for myself. In my relationships, my expectations of men were so high, they were impossible to meet, so inevitably they would all fail me sooner or later.

I desperately had to change, and with the help of someone who specialised in this area, I needed to take a closer look to enable me to understand why I could not handle intimacy on any level, and why I used my body and gave it so freely. Was it that I thought it was all I had to give to a man to make him love me?

Chapter Fifteen

Rehab, Not Ab Fab

Mal agreed to look after my daughter and after a couple of months my funding was sorted out and off I went to get my life sorted once and for all. I was under the impression that the rehab would be like a health farm, kitted out with swimming pools, spas and masseurs, like you read about in women's magazines. As I walked through the door full of high expectations, I observed my surroundings, yes, just how I imagined, the marbled floor with a beautiful waterfall in the centre, the acres of land and woodland were breathtaking, well worth the wait, I thought as I searched for the heated pool. I was approached by two women who told me I needed to check in and that a full medical and examination was required before I was shown my room. I was not amused when I turned to grab my luggage, only to find the same two nosey people rummaging through my belongings. How bloody dare they? My dumbbells – which I packed in case they did not have a gym, which I thought was highly unlikely – were confiscated together with my vitamin tablets which I must have spent thirty or so pounds on. They informed me that I would receive my nutrients through the healthy menu that they provided, they said my dumbbells were a distraction and exercising obsessively, was one of many ways to avoid looking within ourselves !

After asking a member of staff where the pool and spa was, I became the laughing stock of the centre. For the life of me, I had no idea what was so bloody funny about this. Eventually I cottoned on, the entrance pulled me into a false sense of security with its marbled floor and breathtaking waterfall, the rest of the building was just like a massive bed and breakfast, with average furniture, beds made up of the proverbial white sheets tucked under the end of the mattress like they are in a hospital ward. There was worse news ahead, I was sharing a room with a heroin addict just one day away from her last fix, clucking like a chicken in distress and the other roommate was suffering acute hallucinations and was deep in conversation with herself. I think she was bordering on schizophrenia, brought on by excessive alcohol abuse combined with the withdrawals from years of chucking handfuls of painkillers down her neck. It was like a lunatic asylum in there. My thoughts were seriously focusing on getting the hell out of there, pronto! Sleep had always been a problem for me, my insomnia started from way back when I was a child and I was too frightened to sleep for fear of what my parents would do to each other when war broke out on those Saturdays nights. I definitely had no chance of sleeping with the goings on in my room at the centre. I was told by the counsellor there that I was a drug addict. I was having none of that. I did not think, at this time, that taking Valium for ten years made me a drug addict, its not like heroin and cocaine. I kind of came to agree with them begrudgingly when they reduced my Valium down to one five-milligram tablet per night, which was a huge nose dive considering I was averaging about five or so ten milligrams per tablet per night and a whole lot more in the mornings. The withdrawals terrified me; thank God I was in a safe environment. I would have been sectioned for certain if I had to go it alone. There were no television, no newspapers; they made sure there were no distractions that would get in the way of the intense therapy over the next six weeks.

The number one rule was that there was to be no involvement whatsoever with any of the other residents. If you broke the code of conduct more than three times you were out. I was given one-to-one therapy sessions with my counsellor with whom I spoke in-depth about the problems I had with relationships. Even at this point, I found myself flirting with him and not really taking in what he was telling me after a while. I had spent most of my life being an outrageous flirt and was beginning to realise that I could not help myself. I was more interested in trying to make him fancy me. My counsellor could see right through me, which made me feel stupid, so I switched to defence mode. He was not going to make me feel small and stupid, my barriers went up and I told him he was talking rubbish. I would not be told. You probably know what is coming next, yes, you're right, just to show my counsellor, I went and broke the rules. I met a man in there who came in a few days after me. I gathered from our first conversation together that he thought he was above the rest of us peasants in there. He had all the material possessions, his own swimming pool empire, property, fast cars the lot. I politely informed him that material things can be taken away as quick as they come, he did not want to listen when I told him happiness and peace of mind have to come from within. Possessions are only a temporary fix I went on to say, but he was not interested, he would have to find out the hard way like the rest of us.

Within the six weeks there, I formed a relationship with Kriss, a.k.a. Mister Materialistic. I fancied many men in there but eventually gave in to him after weeks of him trying to pursue me. Looking back, I realised I did not fancy him at all, but I wasn't able to say 'no'. The staff became aware what was occurring with us, this is where I get pulled into the office to get my first warning. I was breaking the code of conduct. I was not helping myself. This was the reason I came into rehab. I did not even have the willpower to keep away from men, even as desperate as I was to get help with my deep desire to be loved and accepted.

Looking back, I was blinded to the fact that there were so many things getting in the way and crowding my mind that I never really had the time or the space to really get to know myself. I was so busy running away from myself, distracting my mind by involving myself in other's lives, that I did not give myself the time to focus on what my true needs were, what I really wanted from my life, what I liked, what I didn't like, what made me happy, what was I passionate about. I really never took the time out to think. I was doing exactly the same thing in rehab, I just could not see it. I was told that I should not be in the same company as this man I had just met, and under no circumstance was I to be left alone with him. At the time I could not see what the counsellor's reasons were. Again, I would not be told what to do, my rebellious streak kicked in as usual. I could walk round the grounds with him as long as there was someone else to accompany us. Not a problem, I laughed to myself. We asked another alcoholic who was as devious as us to keep a lookout which enabled us to disappear in the bushes for a bit of slap and tickle. It is pretty clear to me, why I did not reap the benefits of being in rehab. I was fixing my feelings, by turning my attention to Kriss, instead of focusing on myself. This was the reason why I needed to come to rehab in the first place. I received my second warning after being caught walking the grounds with him without an escort. I'd had enough by now, I could not see the point in staying on being told what and what not to do, and this was not what I had bargained for. I finally flipped when the house duties were read out, it was my turn to get up at six-thirty in the morning to wake the residents and to give them time to dress and get down for breakfast. I was leaving.

My opportunity came that same day during a group therapy class. The counsellor and facilitator were talking to us about anger. At this time in my life I didn't think it applied to me, I never saw myself as an angry person. I was obviously in denial. During the group therapy they were pushing and pushing trying to get me angry. I had had enough, I told them to f-off, walked out slamming the door behind me. Maybe they were getting too close to the truth, they could see through my mask which had been a good disguise to hide what I really felt, these people were cleverer than I gave them credit for. An old saying that my mother always told me, *you can fool some people some of the time, but not all the people all of the time*. Looking back I had detached and suppressed my anger so deep down, that I forgot that it was there. I was very forgiving, abnormally so, considering the pain that had been inflicted on me throughout my life, the reality was that I was full of fear and terrified of confrontation.

I decided, after a lot of persuading by the other residents, to stay and stick it out till the end, which I did begrudgingly. I spent Christmas day and Boxing Day in there, it was awful being away from my daughter, especially this time of the year. Kriss did not quite make it to the end of the six weeks, he left Christmas Eve and thought he had it sussed.

I felt that rehab had not been a complete waste of time for me, at least I was weaned off the Valium now and still had AA to help me with my alcoholism. I could not see back then that I was repeating the pattern with the opposite sex, I still had to have a man swinging off my arm to make me feel alive. My six weeks came to an end and off I went home not feeling much better than I did when I first came in. Unfortunately, my behaviour with men continued and things went from bad to worse. I don't suppose I would ever get another chance to go to rehab and not repeat the same behaviour which jeopardised my chances of the help I really did need, but it is obvious to me today that, I was not ready at that time and had a bit more suffering to endure yet.

I had not really given the man I met in there much thought since I came out, I was more concerned with spending my time with my daughter. I attended a few AA meetings, not as many as I should have and was trying to decide what my daughter and I were going to do to celebrate New Year's Eve. My sponsor was going to an AA disco and invited me and my daughter to go with her and her friends. That afternoon I received a phone call from the man I met in rehab, he asked if we would like to go out for a meal with him that evening. It was a toss up to decide what I should do. Unfortunately, we decided to meet up with Kriss and go out for the meal. Worse decision I could have made.

That evening turned out to be one of the most boring nights I have ever had. Kriss was miserable as hell; he had the manners of a pig and about as much personality as a caterpillar. The only thing I was impressed with was his car. Since that evening Kriss was on my case, he pestered me to see him and, to be honest, he was not my cup of tea at all. As usual I gave in; I did not have the courage to say 'no'. Since that night we started dating and like many times before, another relationship hung in the balance of insanity. He told me he was living with an older woman, owned two bungalows and had a thriving swimming pool business which he bragged about the minute he set foot in rehab. He proceeded to enlighten me about how miserable he was in his relationship and spoke about getting her to leave and moving my daughter and me in with him. Warning bells rang in my head. What was the hurry? I thought, this is moving way too fast for me. He even asked me to sell my flat and put the proceeds into paying off his mortgage on one of the bungalows that he lived in. As foolish as I was, the pressure he was putting me under resulted in a visit to my doctor and being prescribed anti-depressants. This says it all really, at this point, I should have run in the opposite direction.

The drama and upheaval in which I unhealthily thrived on all my life led me into yet another merry-go-round of disaster, pain and heartache. I decided to rent my flat out, take my daughter out of school and moved in with him. I was so wrapped up in the chaos of it all, I did not consider for a moment how my daughter was feeling with all the changes that were taking place. She appeared to be happy and excited moving into this lovely home with all the trimmings. Again, I felt like she trusted me in my decision to move in here though she was sad to leave all her friends behind. It makes me feel dreadful to think that I put my happiness before hers and didn't consider how she felt about the changes in her life taking place. How selfish and inconsiderate I was back then. I feel totally ashamed of myself as a mother when I think how self-absorbed I was, how I put my happiness before anybody else's.

In the beginning I enjoyed the luxuries of the material world that I lived in, I was away from home where I have lived all of my life and welcomed a new beginning. We got Sarah into a grammar school; she had to pass an exam to enrol. Kriss would stay up all hours to help her study and prepare her for the exam. She passed with flying colours and got the highest mark ever recorded. It amazes me to think how she could possibly concentrate with all the changes going on around her. I think that maybe this is how she coped, losing herself in her studies took her mind away from the concerns and worries I'm sure she was feeling inside. I took on the role naturally as a Suzy home maker, cleaning and cooking and falling over myself to please. Kriss worked every hour he could with his swimming pool business. We received a call one evening from a guy we met in rehab, he had relapsed and was in a bad way. We decided to drive to Ipswich where he lived to try and help him get back on his feet again. Kriss and I were still sober, which we had been since leaving rehab. We found our friend sprawled on the floor surrounded by sweet wrappers – apparently that is all this guy had eaten in weeks – he was a mental and physical wreck. It was such a sad sight to see, by the grace of God go I, I thought whilst cleaning up his vomit and cleaning the debris which he was surrounded in. We managed to get some food down him, cleaned him up and get him back on his feet again.

Driving back, feeling useful and humble, we decided to divert to the coast to chill out before we headed back. Mum had my daughter for a few days, so there was no need to hurry back. Feeling rather pleased about being Good Samaritans and helping our friend out, I thought it would be nice to relax and have a little drink. The insanity of this illness crept in again. As I mentioned before, my head would try to trick me, telling me this time it will be different. It did not remind me of all the pain and torture I went through each time I tried drinking sensibly. The result was always the same, the drinking got out of control from taking that first sip.

Now the seed had been planted in Kriss' head, we had no chance; just the mention of a drink was all it took. It had been suggested to me many times by others who suffer from this lethal disease that if the thought comes in, do not dwell on it, it is the thinking that starts you drinking. I knew this at this point, but foolishly chose to ignore the warning signs, my mind convinced me, yet again, that it would be different this time. From that moment on, we found ourselves plonked in a bar with large glasses filled with our favourite tipple. This was the beginning of the trail of destruction that lay ahead for us from taking that first drink. We had managed to get thrown out from every single bar we went in. Two raging out-of-control alcoholics on the loose after months of abstinence was a force to be reckoned with.

We found ourselves surrounded by a gang of thugs that fancied their chances. Wow, was I impressed when my boyfriend said he would take the lot of them on. Blow after blow, they fell to the floor like skittles, he came out unscathed without a scratch on him, it was awesome Kriss was a big built stocky man who could hold his own. After witnessing what I thought was a magnificent display of bravery, I began to see Kriss in a different light. I knew at this point why I was with him now, he reminded me of my father, all protecting and mighty. I knew there must have been a reason why I hooked up with him in the first place. There had to have been something that attracted me to him, it had taken a while for the penny to drop. We eventually went back home two days later, after leaving our stamp on the Essex coast.

After abstaining from alcohol since we came out of rehab,(but not attending Alcoholics Anonymous meetings for ongoing support, which is vital to maintain my sobriety), taking that first drink was the beginning of the end, as far as our relationship was concerned. That bender lasted a year and a half. It just goes to show where that first drink can take you, as I was informed many times before, it gets worse never better, and how right those people were.

We were married roughly eight months later, it was a marriage made in hell: two active alcoholics under one roof. How one of us did not kill the other one is beyond belief, it certainly was not for the want of trying, well, especially on my behalf. On the morning of the wedding, my husband-to-be was unbelievably drunk from being up most of the night before. He was so drunk he could not even dress himself. My heart was breaking as I tried everything I could to persuade him to get out of bed and not go back to sleep. The caterers had arrived, the Rolls Royce that we owned was being washed and polished, the best man, who also ran the business with Kriss, was also an alcoholic and paralytic, my best friend and his wife turned up looking absolutely mortified at the sad state this shambolic wedding was turning into.

We managed to get Kriss on his feet and dragged him to the registry office. We were a laughing stock; I could have died from embarrassment, my AA friends who forced themselves along for my sake, looked on bewildered at what they were witnessing. The reception was back at our bungalow. Just when you thought it can't get any worse, the CD player died on us – it just packed in, so now we had no music, my husband had taken off and was nowhere to be found, my mother punched a mutual friend to the floor, for taking the last bottle of Jack Daniels; it was ludicrous. Just to end the day on a perfect note, a couple who were friends of my husband had a mighty great row, jumped in separate cabs and sodded off. I spent all night babysitting an eight month old baby who would not stop screaming and a little girl of five or so who was asking where Mummy and Daddy had gone. When my newlywed husband decided to put in an appearance the next morning, I told him that the marriage was going to be annulled; he had just woken up in the shed at the bottom of our garden, very romantic indeed. I did not follow through my threat of dissolving the marriage and decided to put that dreadful day behind me.

Before long the cracks started to appear, the arguments started, the business was going under, customers were complaining that their swimming pools had not been finished. The reason being that my husband and his partner had spent the money which was given to them for materials to finish the pools on alcohol. The VAT man was screaming out for the tax returns to be sent back, the more the pressure built, the more he drank. The day came when my husband showed his true colours. He rammed my forehead into the bedroom wall and the bump was so big that I could see it sticking out without having to look in the mirror. Things would be thrown and smashed; I would be on the receiving end of his temper on a regular basis now. Life, yet again, was unbearable. I could not move back to my flat, I had just renewed the contract and let it out to my tenants for another year. I was stuck. It got so bad and I was so desperate that I decided to do away with my husband, before he ended up killing me. I thought that the judge would be lenient when he was made aware of my suffering. I was a jibbering wreck, I walked on eggshells from the time I woke up, till the time I retired to bed, my weight was falling off me, I was descending into severe mental illness.

I spent every waking hour planning and plotting until I came up with a plan. My husband loved ice cream, not a night went by without him having to indulge in a very large bowl of his favourite flavour which was, Baileys. I knew we had a large quantity of Antabuse tablets which we both had been prescribed at one point, to help us stop drinking. These tablets were lethal if you took them with alcohol, we were warned that the effects could be fatal. With this in mind, I decided to crush a large handful in to a smooth paste and then mix it with his ice cream; I thought the taste would be disguised by the strong flavour of the ice cream. When he fell asleep one evening, I went to work on my plan. The minute he woke up he would demand his dessert. I sat on the chair, nervously waiting for him to awake. My heart sank when he declined the ice cream that I offered to get for him, he told me he would have it later. Going to bed that night, I knew the time was coming for my suffering to stop, I slept properly for the first time in ages with sheer relief that my nightmare would soon be over.

Next morning my daughter woke me up crying because she had a really bad stomach ache. I nearly died when I asked her if she had eaten anything. My heart nearly came out of my chest when she told me she had helped herself to some of my husband's ice cream during the night. Oh my God, I have poisoned my daughter. How could I take her to hospital and tell them I had laced the iced cream with Antabuse tablets, they would take her away from me? How could I tell them they were meant to kill my husband? I managed to make my daughter throw up, thank God she only had a small quantity, as otherwise this act of insanity could have had severe consequences.

My hopes of ending this excruciating torment that I was in, were not dashed, I came up with plan B. I still had enough Antabuse to do the job, so I thought of a way that would not put my daughter in any kind of danger ever again. I crushed the tablets to a fine paste, mixed with some boiling hot water to enable the tablets to dissolve; I emptied the contents in to the can and offered him a drink. He did not need much persuading as I handed over the already opened can. I could feel the blood draining from my face as he put the can to his lips. To my horror, he launched the can across the other side of the room and headed off to the vodka bottle. That was it; my plan had been ruined, yet again.

One day when Kriss was at work, I decided that if I did not leave then one of us would end up in the cemetery. I gathered clothes, passport, driving licence, etc., made my way to the school to pick my daughter up. My cat had had kittens the night before, so I made a bed out of a cardboard box to put the kittens and mother in. I felt awful moving the kittens, their mother was agitated and was frantically trying to settle her litter. I had no plans and nowhere to go, I found myself pulling up outside my mother's house. I got the kittens settled, put some of my belongings in Mum's back room, told her to look after my daughter and that I would explain later and headed off to a park. The cab driver looked bewildered as he witnessed the upheaval of it all, I paid him and found a spot to sit and take stock.

I could not believe I had finally gotten away from this drunken dangerous man. I know that I have put a lot of the emphasis on my husband's drinking, but I must add I was not totally innocent for I too was actively drinking throughout the seven months of our married life. My insecurities, fears and shortcomings contributed to the madness and the dysfunctional break down of our relationship. But regardless of that, no women should ever have to be on the receiving end of a violent partner and I am one of the few women that has had the courage to leave.

Then reality kicked in hard. Where was I to go? It would not be fair to expect Mum to have us. My husband phoned me and asked what the hell was going on. He did not seem that concerned that I had left him, he made no effort to try to persuade me to come back, not that I ever would in a million years. I had heard through the grapevine a few months previously, that a couple I knew had split up, the woman had moved out which left her ex living in a three-bedroom house all by himself. I happened to still have the house phone number and decided to give him a ring. I arranged to meet up with him to see if there was any chance he could temporarily put my daughter and I up until we could move back into our flat when the contract was up. He was hesitant to do so, for he had met my husband and was frightened of the repercussions if my husband found out where we were living. Using all my charm, I persuaded him and arranged for my daughter and I to move in. Mum kindly agreed to keep my cat and kittens at her house, which was one less thing I had to worry about.

Chapter Sixteen

Me, Myself and I

Brendan was an odd, slightly off the wall character. He liked a drink and was a bit of a know-it-all. He wasn't a popular man and lived a very sad and lonely existence. He had a big heart and, generally, was a good man. He was openly emotional and would be in floods of tears at any mention of cats or the Queen. I sensed that he was unsatisfied with his life and carried a lot of pain around with him. The world he lived in was very small, he had no children, an ex-wife and a job in the printing trade. Besides work and his drinking, he did little else. I think he was glad of the company when we moved in. I knew that he had taken a fancy to me years ago, therefore I had to make it perfectly clear from the start that me moving in was not going to be happy families. The relationship would always be purely platonic, I did not see him in that way whatsoever.

His home was atrocious; I had never seen anything like it in my life. The air was filled with cat hairs, they were everywhere. He had three cats that had the run of the house. They were allowed to go wherever they wanted in the house, the work surfaces in the kitchen being one of them. The house looked like it had not been introduced to a Hoover for years. I doubt the windows had ever been opened; the place smelled of urine, it was vile. Being extremely houseproud, I was revolted by this, but had to be grateful to have had somewhere to stay, beggars can't be choosers.

I eventually managed to get my daughter into a school; this was a very distressing time for my daughter, for she was far more advanced than most people in her class. She also had to deal with yet another major change in her life, I felt so guilty having to put Sarah through all this again, had she not had enough of being pulled from pillar to post. What effect must it have had on her, it really was not fair on her, having to deal with the trail of debris, which was the result of my selfish and impulsive decisions which I had made without thinking of the consequences of my deluded actions.

Being away from my husband was difficult, even though I was relieved, naturally. I was still obsessing over him, and I mistook this for love, as I had done many times before. I spent every waking hour wondering who he was with, the torment was agonising, and I thought it was never going to go away. I drank myself into oblivion for the first few months after I left him,

Brendan, on many occasions found me passed out in the street or outside a pub somewhere. He went out of his way to help me, he was reduced to tears the nights he would stay up with me when I was too drunk to get myself off the living room floor and get myself upstairs to bed. I knew how much my daughter was affected by my self-destruction, but I just could not put the drink down, the reality of this huge mess I had made and all that I had put myself and especially Sarah through, would haunt me forever. Brendan would stay awake all night to keep me company when I was going through the delirium tremens and those awful panic attacks (the ones where you think you're going to die). My appetite was poor, he cooked for me and did everything he could to make me eat, he certainly had not bargained for all this when he accepted me into his home; he really had his work cut out here.

The hurt and disappointment I felt was too much for me to comprehend. I started cutting my arms to take away the pain, this was not the first time I had self-harmed, it had happened on quite a few occasions when I could not cope with the emotional pain in my life. My arms were covered in scars which I felt totally ashamed of. My sanity was hanging on by a thread, physically my body was breaking down as it had been pushed to the max. If I did not do something soon, my life would end prematurely.

I swallowed my pride and found the courage to walk back through the doors of Alcoholics Anonymous. This time I had to concede to my innermost self that I was powerless over alcohol, and my life was and always had been unmanageable, even before the drink took hold of me. I was welcomed back with open arms; it was good to be surrounded by true friends who wanted the best for me. I made a decision to strip myself down to the bone emotionally and let go completely of everything I had fixed on to escape the true realities of life. Besides the obvious addictions to alcohol and drugs, it was my addiction to men that I really battled and refused to let go of – this seemed to have caused me more trouble than the rest. The moment a man entered my life, the alcohol and drugs would not be far behind, they all seemed to follow suit. I decided to give myself a couple of years of celibacy for looking back as far as I could remember, sex was something that I gave so freely away. I had no respect for my body and used it as a weapon to control and manipulate men into getting what I wanted. Having sex was the only way I knew how to express how I felt. It made me feel loved and wanted, I always thought if I pleased men in this department, they would love me and treat me nice. I never imagined in a million years they would love me just for who I really was. In hindsight, how could they? I never really let them get to know the real me, I couldn't for I never gave myself the freedom, space and the opportunity. I decided I would have no involvement whatsoever with the opposite sex, I needed to get to know who I really was. I knew this would not be an easy ride for someone with my history in the relationship department.

I threw myself into the meetings; I stepped inside of the boat this time around, instead of being a spectator, hovering around on the edge. I practised the twelve step programme, which gave me the tools to handle sobriety. I began a step at a time, practising assertiveness, I could never say 'no' as I mentioned before, if I did, there would be a long drawn-out justification, for fear of not being liked. I had entered this journey of discovery with a different approach, I was eager to learn this time, and as much as I detested being told some home truths, I took it on the chin because ignoring or denying it would have kept me trapped in this horror story.

Changing my attitude was tough, I had been programmed to be the way I had been all my life. I learned that I had a long way to go. I had to learn discipline, I had never played by the rules. In my life, rules were made to be broken, that was my philosophy. I found, at times, the journey rather exciting, taking risks I would never have dreamed of and never had the courage to do without my huge glass of alcohol. I realised that playing the big shot was bloody hard work, trying to keep up my image of happy-go-lucky Gaynor, always laughing and acting the fool, sorting everyone's life out for them was exhausting. To mind my own business was difficult, I had to know the ins and outs of everyone and everything. But it was a relief to sit back and just let them be. I did not realise minding my own business could be so freeing, until I realised I was left with myself.

To keep busy, I decided to make use of my time and redecorate the whole of Brendan's house; I was a dab-hand at painting and decorating, through watching my father work as a child. To be honest, the whole building needed knocking down and starting from scratch. I had two motives for this: one, I thought it would be a nice gesture to show my appreciation for letting me stay there, and two, I had to make it liveable for myself and my daughter. It took me a whole year to decorate. I threw everything out of that house for it was infested with flees and God knows what, my controlling side took over as usual. Five months into recovery, I felt that empty hole inside of me yearning to be filled and the loneliness was crippling. I would cry buckets and hold my knees up towards my chest and rock back and forwards trying to comfort myself, I was a pitiful sight.

In order to put my mental and emotional health first, I had to detach from certain people in my life, at this stage of my recovery. This included family, for my mother was still a drinker and, on occasion, would call me up and try to get me to go over to her house and drink with her. In the past, I had done so on many occasions, which resulted in her turning on me after a good few brandys. I found this really distressing and would leave there in bits. Drink did not agree with Mum, it would bring out her anger and resentments. I found it extremely difficult to detach from my mother. She had helped me through so much in my life and was there to help me pick up the pieces of the mess I had made of my life. It must have been so upsetting for Mum to watch from a distance and witness her daughter destroying her life and feel so powerless to do anything about it. It really hurt me separating myself from her, for she was my mum and I loved her. I don't think Mum understood my decision to keep away until I felt strong enough to go and see her, regardless of whether she was drinking. I tried to explain to her about my alcoholism, but I feel unless you acknowledge the problem, and have a clear understanding of what alcoholism is all about, it is very difficult to see where I was coming from and why I had to do what I had to do to stay sober. I tried to explain to her that I had to be selfish, that my recovery had to be number one on my list of priorities, for if I didn't, I would inevitably drink again.

Mum was unhappy and discontented throughout her life. She had been through a lot and, like so many of us, she suffered terribly as a child. Her mother was a very cold, rigid and bitter woman who showed no love and affection towards her children. She was emotionally unavailable. I harboured deep-rooted anger and resentment towards my mother for the way I was brought up for years. After having intense therapy to overcome my childhood damage, and after a lot of research and remembering the stories Mum told me over the years about her childhood, I realised that Mum and Dad were guilty but not to blame. They had done the best they could raising their children, regardless of the drinking and violence that occurred within the marriage which affected each and every one of my siblings in one way or another.

I had been sober and clean from drugs for eighteen months now; life was the best it had ever been. I was experiencing peace of mind for the first time in my life, I had very few dramas throughout my day. I would retire at night without my mind racing a hundred miles an hour. I could not wait to sleep, and was excited and eager to face a brand new day. I realised how much of my life I had wasted, and that I could never get it back. I was frightened that I would not have much time to do all the things I wanted, for there was so much of life I wanted to see. I became aware of the beauty that surrounded me: how blue the sky was, how beautiful the stars were at night, nature in all its glory. I had never really noticed this before.

My flat became vacant, my lodgers moved out. I could have moved back at this point. Part of me did not really want to go back, for there were too many bad memories of the suffering that took place there. I spoke to Brendan and suggested that if I sold my property, maybe I could pay the rest of his mortgage off and part-own his property. I was living on next-to-nothing, and decided I would be able to pay my debts off, buy a new car and take a holiday. The flat was eventually sold. I put some money in an ISA for my daughter, bought a sports car, had a holiday abroad with my daughter, and treated my twin to a holiday in the Caribbean. I made sure most of my siblings and my mother had something from the sale of my flat. It felt good to give, better than receiving.

I noticed Brendan was drinking more than he used to, he appeared to have adopted a bit of an attitude since I sold my flat, I guess he thought I was beholden to him now. To make matters worse, he told me he was in love with me and always had been. This became a problem. He would not get it into his head that I did not want to be with him, no matter what I said. He was hell-bent on thinking he would eventually change my mind. I began to regret my decision to sell my home; I was stuck now and was irritated by his irrational behaviour. I was basically a glorified house-keeper to him. He was the untidiest man I have ever known, my tolerance level was declining big time, and eventually I could not stand to be in the same room as him.

Chapter Seventeen

The Hand of the Devil

I was approaching the end of my second year in recovery and was still celibate (this was a miracle on its own). I had changed a lot in those two years, by now I had reached a place where I was beginning to feel comfortable inside my own skin, and had a very good insight into who I really was. A week before the end of my second year in recovery, I was at my mother's and she introduced me to her new lodger. He was dark and pretty rough looking although there was something mysterious about him that intrigued me. I mentioned to Mum that I found him attractive and she only went and told him! I was so embarrassed. He asked Mum for my phone number, without thinking I gave it to him, and thought no more of it. Weeks later he decided to call, I was a gibbering wreck, I did not have my large glass of confidence now, this was a brand new ball game, I was like a dumb-struck teenager, making small talk about absolute nonsense.

He was aware I was in recovery, but asked me out for a drink never the less. Being sober and on my own all this time, I thought by now, I am strong enough to go out socialising amongst all you 'normal folks'. I had stayed away from people and places where there was alcohol but I was ready to face the world, armed with my new coping skills and a whole new outlook towards life. I was ready to go.

Making an extra special effort with my appearance, off I went in my car, heading toward Mother's house where I was to meet him. As I pulled out onto the main road, my heart was beating faster than normal and I began to panic – I needed some courage, I could not do this sober. I did not have the courage to go on a date; I felt like a virgin, a terrified school girl. What would I talk about? Would he find me interesting? All these questions were spinning around in my head. I did not feel comfortable being sober, I did not know how to act for I had always drank especially when going on a date – I could be whoever I wanted, the alcohol took all the fears away. Like I had done many times before, I kept this thought of a drink in my head long enough, until the mental obsession overtook me. Before long, I was swigging back from a bottle of hooch. Everything I had been through, all the work I had put into my recovery was a distant memory.

We ended up in a bar in Ruislip. I must have thought that I could handle being in a bar, for surely he would like a drink. I justified my reason for being in the bar. I most probably thought that I would be okay, but I was fooling myself. I so desperately needed a drink to overcome the craving, that I had no mental defence against taking that next drink, it was out of my control. I ordered a coke to try and fight against this compulsion, my body was screaming out for more alcohol, it was torture. I had to leave the bar, my head was in turmoil, and I suggested we head back to Mum's.

She was in bed when we arrived. I was offered a joint and thought smoking might take away the obsession to drink. Obviously it didn't and before long I begged him to go and buy a bottle. I could not take much more. I did not want to drink but I needed to, my body was screaming out for that next drink, I had no control whatsoever. I called this man, Damien, you will understand why later. I spent the next week with him, he stayed over at mine, we smoked dope day in day out, I had been drinking since the first night I met him. I had fallen by the wayside, I could not see the wood for the trees, my meetings were thrown in the river alongside my hopes and dreams for the future. All I cared about was this one magical person that had entered my life, I ate and drank him, and he was the focus of my world.

One evening he decided that we should stay in a bed and breakfast for the night in Harrow. He stocked up on the vodka and cigarettes, locked me in our room and told me to stay there, he would be back shortly. Whilst he was gone, I helped myself to three quarters of the bottle of vodka, and by the time he came back I was absolutely hanging, bearing in mind I had not drank alcohol for nearly two years. Through the haze, I noticed he pulled out some kind of substance that I did not recognise, I asked him what it was, he told me it was a nice little magical parcel, especially for me. He put this substance on some foil, and asked me to put an empty pen tube in my mouth and take in the substance. I did not have a clue what I was taking; it made me feel sick. After a while, I noticed I could not move, I was spaced out of my mind. I could see him looking down at me with a huge sickly grin on his face. I eventually managed to get on my feet. He took me to a bar, I remember I was so out of it that I could not work out how to open a packet of crisps. I found myself at his mercy. Throughout that night, he continued to make me take this substance.

The next morning, we left the bed and breakfast. I had to be held up, for my legs were too weak to carry me. Again, I questioned what I had taken, but he just laughed like a lunatic. En route back he told me he was going to pick something up to give me some energy, which I welcomed for I felt terrible. I waited nervously in the car, I felt uneasy, and this multi-storey council estate looked like something you would see in the Bronx in New York. There were men and women hanging out on the corner of the block, like they were waiting to do a drugs deal. Damien returned to the car with a rock of crack cocaine, which was a new one on me. He put the rock in his mouth, in case we got stopped by the police, in which case he would swallow it, it was wrapped in layers of cellophane, and therefore, he could pass it out the other end, still in one piece.

Mum was out getting her hair done, so we had the house to ourselves. Damien made a pipe out of an empty coke bottle. I watched with eager eyes to see how this was done, I could not wait to take this as long as it made me feel better and stimulated my energy levels, which were, by now, on the floor. I inhaled this substance and kept it down as long as I could as I was told to. My God, I had never experienced this feeling of euphoria in my life, it was heaven to me, from that moment on I was hooked on crack cocaine.

Damien spent most of his time at mine, in between working as a controller and cab driver. He kept giving me those magical parcels which he first produced that night at the bed and breakfast every waking hour. By the time I realised it was heroin he was pumping into me, it was too late, I was hooked, which was his intention from the start. Over the next year, I became a prisoner in my own bedroom. The bastard had me just where he wanted. He would make me smoke this lethal drug the minute my eyes opened and then would leave me to go to work, knowing that I was unable to function. He would check on me at lunch time, to give me more, to keep me grounded until he came home in the evening. If I complained, he would put his hands round my throat and threaten to kill me. He was completely insane, he terrorised the life out of me. I looked like a waif, I had lost so much weight, and I had no fight left in me. One morning I waited for him to go to work, I had to get away from him. I managed to get in my car, I could not see properly, everything was fuzzy, I could just about hold the steering wheel. As I was getting to the top of my road, I noticed there was a car parked that would not let me through to get out on to the main road. I turned the car around and tried to get out the other end of the road, this also was blocked by a car. Damien had got two of his cronies from the cab firm to spy on me and prevent me from getting away.

Brendan could hear the screams coming from my bedroom during the night when Damien would hit me. He banged on my bedroom door one night and told Damien to leave me alone, and he also was frightened of him. I had another attempt to get away from this evil vile man; I grabbed my daughter one day and headed for the park. He called me from outside my house and threatened to smash the door down if I did not let him in. He was not aware I was not in the house. I got another call, after he smashed the door down, he told me that when he found me he was going to kill me. I suppose you're wondering why I did not go to the police at this stage, basically, I was too frightened of the repercussions. He was too deranged, he thought he was above the law. When I eventually came back, I got the hiding of my life; he always hit me where it did not show, like most cowards do.

Something had to be done, before it was too late, I suggested to Damien that we should both try to come off the heroin, we should go together to a walk-in drugs and alcohol centre, to see what they could do to help us. Damien told me to say I was on more heroin than I was already taking, which was a hell of a lot, so that they would give me a high dosage of methadone, which is a substitute for heroin, which would keep me pretty sedated and weak. Obviously, I was yet again ignorant to that fact. Damien continued to take heroin together with his prescribed methadone. I pretended to take down the heroin he forced me to have, I needed to come off this shit I was addicted to; I hated it with a vengeance. This twisted psychopath even mixed some heroin in the crack we also smoked, which I knew nothing about, he did this to try and get me kicked off the methadone programme I was on. When I had my two week regular check up at the clinic, they found heroin in my urine. I had no idea that he was doing this. I was told if it happened again, I would no longer be treated at the clinic and my prescription for methadone would be stopped. The withdrawals were horrific, it felt like every muscle and bone in my body ached. I thought the itching and the hot and cold sweats would never pass. If I was like this on methadone to help with the withdrawals, how the hell do people go it alone and do cold turkey?

I tried to finish with Damien on numerous occasions but he would follow me everywhere I went. He would attack me in the street, force me into his car and sexually assault me. I could not continue being victimised and the only way I could survive was to run away. I had to explain to my daughter, not the true extent of my suffering to spare her feelings, but told her I had to go away for a while to sort myself out. It tore me apart having to leave her with a friend, but it was my only chance of getting clean and away from this monster. At least if I was away from him, it would give me time to get my strength back and then to figure out what I am going to do, for I had to return eventually, to be with my daughter.

I told my landlord and Sarah where I was going. I swore them to secrecy as the last thing I needed was for Damien to hunt me down. I stayed with a friend who lived on the East Coast. I found a clinic that continued my methadone programme, which was reduced every couple of weeks. I lived on my nerves for fear of being found. I informed the local police station of my predicament, who reassured me they were only a phone call away. My daughter came to visit me, which kept my morale up and reinforced the reason why I needed to get clean, get my confidence back and toughen up. I was determined to go to any length to stand up to this parasite once I returned home, armed with nerves of steel.

The loneliness and being separated from my daughter was immense, I had been away for months now and was coming to the end of my methadone treatment. I knew it was nearly time to come home, it felt great to be able to think clearly, and have some control back in my life. When I reflected back over the past couple of years, I could hardly absorb the predicament I had got myself in. After having two years in recovery and getting my life in order, I was struggling to come to terms with where I had ended up. It just goes to show what taking that first drink can do.

When I arrived back to Ruislip, I had gained a few pounds in weight and was completely free of methadone. I was slightly nervous, naturally, but the girl who fled, broken and bruised, returned with sheer determination to tackle life head on, particularly any trouble from Damien. Fortunately, his cab firm had gone bust and Damien had moved out of the area. I was free of him at last, my nightmare was now over.

Chapter Eighteen

From Looney to Uni

During the time I spent away from home, I could not drink a large quantity of alcohol as, combined with the methadone, it made me nauseous. I hate to add that I certainly made up for lost time, the minute I stepped back onto London soil. You would think, by now, that I would have thrown the towel in when it came to relationships, but no. I had to travel down a few more floors of the lift, and gather some more baggage along the way first. It seemed like my behaviour would continue until I took my last breath. My self-will was running riot, and nothing less than a psychic change would stop this trail of destructive behaviour. Why through my wisdom of years and suffering did I not have the inner ability to change? Had I not suffered enough?

It is ludicrous to say, but yet again I got involved with someone else. I was a relationship addict, I heard that sick attract sick and I believe this to be true; this definitely seems to be the case with me anyhow. He was an alcoholic and drug addict, my God, I cringe writing this, and here we go again, off on the merry-go-round of insanity. As you do, we spent most of our time together, drinking, taking drugs, fighting, and making up – all the usual nonsense that is part and parcel of this self-defeating behaviour. I funded our drinking and drug taking habit, for I still had a couple of thousand left out of the proceeds of the sale of my flat. I was being robbed under my own nose, but was too out of it to notice. I would give him my cash card to draw money out for crack cocaine, every time he made a withdrawal, he would take a little extra out for himself. This went on for months, until one morning I opened a letter from the bank, saying that I had gone over my limit. My credit card was also up to the max, this little bastard had wiped me out. Once the funds had run out, so did he. I eventually ended up having a meeting with the official receiver, I was bankrupt.

Licking my wounds, resentments oozing out of every pore in my body, I was riddled with self-hatred for what I had put myself and my daughter through. I had to do something constructive with my life; I had wasted so many years, would I ever see a light of hope at the end of this long, dark and dismal tunnel? I thought I would put my experiences of life to good use and had a notion I could be of help to others who were struggling with life just like I had. I was not aware at this moment in time that I had to overcome the errors of my ways, before I could help others, but my heart was in the right place, I enrolled in a counselling course.

★★★

Walking into the classroom, I was filled with fear and terror, just like I felt at my first day at school. I had forgotten what a terrifying ordeal school was for me, especially as I was an underachiever and, thanks to my mother's programming, believed I was thick. To make matters worse, when we were told to introduce ourselves to the other students, who all seemed to have interesting careers unlike myself, I stood up and said, 'My name is Gaynor, and I am an alcoholic,' I was so used to saying that at my AA meetings, it just came out, well, the embarrassment I felt was excruciating, what a bloody start that was, I had broken my own anonymity there and then. I had set myself up, right there and then, how am I going to cover up my hangovers in the future here on this course? They would be watching my every move.

Halfway through the course, I had run out of excuses for not turning up, even if my excuses were genuine, they inevitably thought it was down to my drinking. I basically had to quit before I got thrown off the course. A year later, I returned and completed my year with a certificate in Person-Centred Counselling, by the skin of my teeth.

My home life living under the same roof as my landlord ,Brendan, was like *One Flew Over the Cuckoo's Nest*. His behaviour was disturbing; he was a liability to himself and others around him. He made Frank Spencer look intelligent. His drinking and crack cocaine habit, (which I, too, must admit to participating in), was turning his mind to mush and this was having an effect on his work and our friendship. On a couple of occasions, he nearly burned the house down: he had put his dinner in the oven, drank a bottle of wine and fallen asleep. If I had not been awake, I hate to think what would have happened. He would also wake up in the night disorientated, entering my bedroom, not being able to remember where he slept. One night he got up in the early hours of the morning and I found him wandering down the street stark bloody naked. He told me he was meeting his work-friend to load the lorry up!

Things got so bad that I was frightened to go to sleep at night, in fear of what he would do next. I had to protect myself. I had to take the plug off the chain in the bathroom sink, to stop him from flooding the place. Many a time he would get up again in the middle of the night, put the plug in the sink, run the tap and then go back to bed forgetting what he had done. I had to put the chub lock on the front door and steal his key to prevent him from wandering around the street naked in the night.

Brendan was a compulsive liar; taking responsibility was something he could not do. Paying bills did not apply to him as far as he was concerned. The bailiffs had served papers on him, the house was going to be repossessed if he did not pay the loan he took out, using his house as collateral.

My daughter was coming on in leaps and bounds, and was studying hard for her A-levels. She passed all her exams with flying colours; she had made her mind up years ago that she wanted to work in Law. She had a wealth of friends and was loved by everyone. It is hard not to like her; she is kind, loving and caring, beautiful and full of life. The day came when I had to let her go—she was off to University. It broke my heart to say my goodbyes and leave her there. As I walked out of the gates, I felt like I had lost my right arm; we were the best of friends. Now that I was left by myself, I had to take stock and decide what I was going to do with my life.

I thought this time is as good as any to concentrate on a career in counselling. I already had my certificate, which would help me get on a diploma course. I enrolled at a university, terrified out of my mind. Was I out of my depth? Those words Mum used to say, 'thick,

thick, thick', went round in my head and those feelings of not being good enough came flooding back. I had not written an essay since I left school, I was thrown into confusion when we were asked to do it Harvard style. What on earth did that mean? I was too embarrassed to ask. I felt so inferior compared to the other students; most of them had been to university before and found the written work a breeze, whereas I struggled. They had high-powered careers where I had not. I thought my tutors would eventually discover that I was not up to the standard of work that was required and ask me nicely to leave. My essays came back many times with feedback that upset me, I was just not getting it, and I felt like the dunce of the classroom.

A few months into the course, I started to settle a little. I linked up with another student who I felt comfortable with; we had a lot in common and a shared sense of humour. We giggled in class like two naughty schoolchildren; I had a lot of fun with him, which eased the pressure I was putting myself under. I had a placement which was part of the course requirement, to do one hundred hours of one-to-one counselling with supervision. My confidence seemed to grow when I discovered that I was much more competent with my counselling skills than I was with the written assignments I had to do. Through my own experiences empathy came naturally when working with my clients. My work was rewarding, I was given the chance to help people less fortunate than myself. I worked in a day centre for adults who were disabled or had learning difficulties. It certainly put a few things into perspective for me, and made me realise how fortunate I was. My boss praised me for the work I was doing and my supervisor gave me a glowing report of my progress as a trainee counsellor. Over time, I started to see myself in a different light, I realised I had the potential to become a good counsellor. My assignments were coming together and my feedback was becoming more positive, I was amazed when reading my final report from my boss at the day centre, that he stated I was a 'true professional'. This may have not meant much to others, but it meant a lot to me, especially with the negative programming I had growing up. By now, I had started to believe in myself and my abilities, this was something I only could have dreamed of many years ago. Two years had flown by; I can't say that I truly enjoyed the experience at university, for me it was an uphill struggle. The most important thing to have come out of this experience, was that I gained a diploma and, at long last, smashed the concept in my mind that I was a 'thick' person. I felt rather the opposite actually, I now believe I can achieve anything I want in life, as long as I put my mind to it, anything is possible.

Chapter Nineteen

A Brave New World

My daughter graduated from university with a law degree and I was the proudest mother in the world. I sobbed with happiness watching her step onto the stage with her gown and hat on. It was the happiest day of my life, especially looking back at all that we had been through together. She is now just a few months away from being a fully qualified solicitor.

During the time at Uni, I attended AA meetings and managed to stay clean. I felt that during my life I had started so many things, but never seen them through. My addictions had prevented me from doing so much, alcohol and drugs are the biggest thieves of all, they took away so many things that I held dear to me. I was determined, this time, that my addictions would not get in the way. I intended to take this opportunity I so desperately wanted and had worked so hard for; I was going to see this through right to the end.

My friendship with Roger, whom I met at uni, developed into a loving relationship. He was kind and gentle, a very spiritual man with a heart of gold. He had emotional baggage like most of us and was not perfect but he was intelligent and had a passion for life. He eventually moved in with me, for he had nowhere to live and was separated from his wife and going through a messy divorce. Things moved very quickly with us, it seemed to be working and yes, I was happy.

The atmosphere in my house was terrible, Brendan did not take kindly to my new boyfriend, I sensed he still held a torch for me. Brendan did not own the property any more, for it had been bought by the loan company, time was running out if he was going to buy it back. People were forever knocking on the door, trying to retrieve the debt that had mounted up over time. My partner and I were going to be made homeless; we were struggling to find a place to rent that allowed pets. I had a beautiful German Shepherd which I adored with all my heart, he was my best friend and soul mate, there was no way on earth was I going to get rid of him. We searched every letting agency we could, trying to find somewhere to live. We had managed to save some money, just enough for a deposit to put down, thank God, we would have been out on the streets otherwise.

The day came when the new owner came in to change the locks and take over the house. I cried like a baby, I hated endings and was still terrified of change. I had been living in this house for eleven years, even though my time here was difficult, with Brendan's shenanigans, it still was hard to say goodbye. Fortunately, a few months previously, we had managed to find a one bedroom flat by the sea. All my life I have wanted to live by the sea and my dream came true. The flat was a stone's throw from the sea, and it was beautiful. It was not the most ideal situation; we were on the top floor with no garden for my dog, but we were just so grateful to have a roof over our head.

Nobody, not even my family knew I had moved or where I moved to. The sad part of this is that I had lived in Ruislip, Middlesex for forty-seven years, yet there was nobody of any relevance to say goodbye to, which says it all really. I even kept the move secret from Mum for the time being, I needed to get sorted out and settled first.

To be honest, before departing from Ruislip, I still was finding it difficult to abstain from my addictions, little did my partner realise that by running around trying to look after me when I was withdrawing, feeding me and getting me that morning drink, he was enabling me to continue. I would drink knowing that I would not be alone in my suffering during the aftermath of my binges. It was a while until he realised the extent of my addictions, and how severe it was. The woman he saw with a drink in her hand the night before, laughing and joking, not a care in the world was a far cry from the shaking, gibbering wreck who was too weak to walk to the bathroom without assistance the next morning. It broke his heart. The shame and the guilt was crippling, the embarrassment was pitiful until I drank enough to stop the shakes and the false reality kicked back in again.

Before joining the motorway, I took in all my surroundings: the memories, the people, everything around me that had been my life here since I was born. I had mixed emotions (some sad, some happy), the anticipation of the unknown and what lay ahead of me, and the pain of the past I was finally leaving behind. Someone told me years ago when I was a teenager, that if I didn't ever get out of Ruislip I would be swallowed up and not have a chance in life; those words became the truest words ever to be spoken.

During the first week we had moved in, we were busy unpacking and getting things sorted out. This place was not alien to me; I had come to this area many times as a child, and knew my way around pretty much. This is one of the reasons why I chose to come to the East Coast; it was only an hour and a half drive away to get back to London. I did not realise what an impact moving out of Ruislip would have on me. I sunk into depression, my nerves were shot to pieces and I was homesick already. It was not that I was missing my family and friends back home, I hardly had any contact with my family and friends, I had none, the people who came into my life in Ruislip were drinking buddies, nothing else. I am now fortunate to have a few real friends, who I love and trust dearly; unfortunately they live in different parts of the country, but are only a phone call away.

As I said, I found it hard to settle, and had to give myself time to adjust. The property was so small, I could not breathe; I felt claustrophobic. It was so small that my poor dog had to walk backwards, for the rooms were too small for him to turn around. Not having a garden was a huge problem, I had to take him out as many times as I could, it was such a pain having to get up early in the morning and take him out last thing at night before bed. Getting down the stairs was difficult, not very good for his back legs which some German Shepherds have problems with as they get older. My partner is partly disabled and has to use a stick; obviously this did not do him any favours either.

We had moved at the end of December, the wind was bitter here, being situated right on the sea front, it was the coldest winter we had had for years. The ocean view out of the window in the flat was breathtaking and lying in bed at night listening to the waves smashing against the sea wall was glorious. Waking up to the sound of the seagulls and checking to see if the sea was still there was something I did for months, I was frightened it would disappear. Regardless of all the beauty of nature surrounding me, I still felt miserable, terribly lost and frightened. I would walk my dog along the front at night and would not see a single soul. You would hardly see a light on in the row of shoreline bungalows. Most people who lived here were elderly and lights were out before darkness fell, they were tucked up in their beds. It was like God's waiting room. The village was five minutes away, there were plenty of fish and chip shops scattered about, plenty of pubs to drink in and a few novelty shops. In the summer they made their money with the holidaymakers, but God knows how they survived in the winter months, mind you, many didn't – a lot of the businesses collapsed and shut down.

People appeared to be friendly enough; a polite hello was refreshing when out and about with my dog. Very different from London, where people are too busy rushing around to take time to notice anything else going on around them. The pace of life here was very different, people walked around like they were in a trance-like state. I put it down to the sea air in the beginning, now I am not so sure, strange people indeed, some looked like they had given up on life and thrown the towel in.

The activities in this small community left a lot to be desired – if you were seventy or over, the world was your oyster, if you were younger, you'd had it. Everyone knew everybody, if you stepped into the pub, after five minutes you would know everyone and their business. If you kept yourself to yourself like my partner and I had since we moved here, you were treated like an outsider and basically ignored. This suited me fine, I cannot get involved with idle gossip and small talk, it is not who I really am or how I choose to live.

I was having terrible trouble trying to adapt to this way of life. Not long after I moved, I felt like there was a huge hole inside of me that needed to be filled. I had spent my life surrounded by people bringing trouble to my door, alcoholics and drug dealers bringing family feuds and unhealthy relationships. I could not walk to the local shop without bumping into ex-boyfriends or the barflies I used to drink with, there was no getting away from them. I had no peace of mind, inside or outside of my home. I guess the discomfort I was feeling, was down to being alone with myself, away from the distractions and the madness of everyday life, this feeling was something I had not experienced before.

As painful as this was, I did not drink to avoid the emotional turmoil I was in, something was changing within me, I can't explain what, and I stayed with the feelings, hoping they would come to pass. My partner was very supportive during this time, he reassured me that it was early days and that my reaction to trying to adjust and familiarise myself with my new surroundings was quite normal. A few months had passed and things were settling down, my mood lifted, I was starting to appreciate the tranquillity and the essence of the beauty that surrounded me. Being able to go anywhere I chose without anyone knowing who I was or pointing their finger, being anonymous was something I loved. For the first time in my life, I can honestly say, my mind was peaceful, not racing on full throttle a hundred miles an hour. My everyday life started to become manageable. The simplicity of just living in the here and now and not planning my whole life ahead, was a major breakthrough. I reflected back through my life, now that I was away from all the insanity, a clear picture was emerging of the reality of my existence. I had been trapped and surrounded by people who had never had my best interest at heart; they would take and keep taking, till I had nothing more to give. It was only when all my emotional, mental and physical energy had been squeezed out of me, and I had nothing left to give, that I found myself, as always, alone and distraught. In hindsight, I have never really protected my own wellbeing and made it my top priority, this has been the crux of most of my problems. The endless times I have put myself in the same old position, helping others, regardless of how it was affecting me, I paid the price every single time, the end result always led me back to the bottle.

Moving was a new beginning for me, and it has turned out that this move was the best gift I could ever give to myself, I now had the chance to become all that I could be. The freedom and space gave me the opportunity to re-evaluate my life and to work out what was important to me and what I wanted out of life. I was in no hurry to find work in the counselling field, my wellbeing had to come first. I would not be of any use to others until my own life was in order. I have had many opportunities to exercise self-restraint since I have been here, especially when it comes to helping others. I have had to take a good few steps backwards and only take on what I can handle. I am learning to understand that I have to let go and let others make their mistakes and learn life's harsh lessons the way I had to. After spending so many years trying to control people and situations, I realised that I could only help people who helped themselves, and this self-defeating behaviour had always resulted in me sabotaging my own happiness and recovery.

Chapter Twenty

Best Legs in Heaven

It had been three months since I had moved here, my life was pretty simple and the dust was settling. I received a phone call from my daughter saying my mother was not well, she was diagnosed with cancer of the ovaries. Mum had overcome cancer of the bowel some time back, but unfortunately the cancer had returned and had spread. My peace of mind evaporated that instant and was replaced by fear and overwhelming sadness. Mum was offered chemotherapy which would buy her a little more time. I was informed that Mum only had six months to live. I could not take this in. I thought Mum would live forever, this was too much for me to digest, the thought of Mum not being here literally made me sick. Mum put on a brave face and avoided anything to do with her diagnosis. She was in great pain and had lost her appetite, Mum loved her food, and she was not eating enough to keep a sprat alive, and was losing weight rapidly.

I drove down to London to see her, I was terrified, all the memories of when Dad got ill and the loss of him came flooding back after all these years. My heart broke in two when I saw Mum, she looked like Dad did before he passed away. I could see that the cancer was eating her up, she was skin and bones. Her eyes had sunken back in their sockets; her cheek bones poked through the thin layer of skin on her face. I could not get my head around this at all. I cannot describe the pain, only people who have lost someone dear to them can know how it feels. I stayed at Mum's, I knew I was not strong enough to handle this and my mind was screaming out for someone or something to take the emotional pain away, I couldn't lose Mum, but there was nothing I could do to stop this from happening. My twin sister took a long spell off from work to take care of Mum. My younger brother had no chance of coping, he was so dependent on Mum, and she was always there for him, no matter what.

Mum was put on morphine to control the pain, the hallucinations were horrific, and Mum was losing control of her bowels and had to have a catheter. She was such a proud women, it must have been hell for her to be reduced to this, and I would not wish what Mum went through on anybody, what a terrible way to end your life. My brother, sister and I watched over Mum. The times we thought we had lost her, were soul-destroying. I had been staying at Mum's for a few days, I could not sleep, I felt I was losing my mind, the fear crippled me, my sister and brother were also in pieces. I had to go back home, for my sanity was hanging on by a thread, but to leave my mum, knowing I would not see her alive again was incredibly painful. The drive back was a hazy blur, I vaguely remember most of the journey. I was numb.

I picked up a drink when I returned, I could not cope, and I knew drink was not the answer, it was not going to change anything, but my world had fallen apart. The dreaded day came when I received a phone call saying Mum had died. My sister and brother were with her, they said her last hours were horrific; she struggled to get her breath. Why could she not have gone peacefully in her sleep, why did she have to suffer right until the end? Mum had suffered most of her life, having to end her life still in pain seemed so unfair.

The funeral was one of the saddest days of my life, the last time I felt this deep sense of loss was when I buried my father. I felt detached, like it was not real. It was like watching the saddest play I have ever seen with my mother playing the starring role, but was not present with the remaining cast after the en core.

Once back home again, I knew I could not continue drinking. Continuing to put alcohol on top of my emotions would have finished me off. My mother would not have wanted that, she knew how much I had battled with my addictions. Her strength and her courage, right up until the end of her life, remained with me. To experience the overwhelming grief and every human emotion present, without anaesthetising myself with alcohol or drugs was beyond belief.

Days and weeks passed slowly, the grief absorbed every part of my body; I was lost in a sea of doom. I must have cried more tears in those three months than I ever had since I lost my father back in 1979. My mind and my heart could not accept or process Mum not being here anymore. Nothing made sense to me at all. I questioned my existence and I realised how short life really is. Where do we all go to when we die? What if it truly is the end? Is there really a God, or had I been praying to nobody all this time? All these questions occupied my every waking hour and the thought of never seeing my parents again turned my stomach.

My partner tried his upmost to comfort me, it hurt him deeply to see the pain I was in. I withdrew from everything and everybody, except for my dog. He was my comforter and motivator, he could comfort me in ways others couldn't; he was my soulmate who gave me his love unconditionally. I knew it was early days and people were right in saying time is a healer, but when you are in that black tunnel, it seems you will never see the light of day again.

I spoke to Mum every minute of the day, pleading with her to let me know she was still around in the spiritual world. I asked for just a little sign to relieve me from my suffering. One evening I had returned home after taking my dog out and when I walked into my bedroom my mum's little fluffy dog which I had taken after she passed away was on the floor. She had this little dog on the top of the settee where she always used to sit. I had placed the dog high on top of my wardrobe and there was no way it had just fallen down. I picked it up and placed it back where it was before.

The next evening, I was sitting watching the television, when my dog came in looking a bit sheepish; he had the fluffy dog in his mouth. I felt this overwhelming sense that we were not alone, as much as I tried to rationalise this incident, it still seemed a bit uncanny. Since then, there have been other strange occurrences taking place in our home. My partner and I were sitting in the bedroom one evening and, right in front of our very eyes, objects came flying off my dressing table. I was convinced Mum was trying to let me know she was still around.

After these strange occurrences, my grief lessoned slightly, I felt a sense of comfort and reassurance knowing that Mum and Dad's spirits were still alive. These occurrences surely could not be coincidences, there did not seem to be a logical explanation. Unfortunately, this sense of reassurance faded and I was back there again, my whole being consumed with never-ending grief and despair.

CHAPTER TWENTY ONE

A NEW BEGINNING

Since I was a child, I have always prayed. My parents were not religious people but I always remember Mum saying 'Jesus is listening' when she knew I was telling a lie. I went to Sunday school and would read from *The Children's Bible*, but that was about it. When I joined AA, I learned to pray for strength and courage, for my needs to be met, rather than what I wanted in life. I came to see that I could not remove my obsessions with alcohol and drugs and that I needed help from something or somebody a lot more powerful than I was. I chose to call this higher power God, and that was my understanding of Him. I begged and pleaded with God to help me accept the passing of my mother and for the strength and courage to carry on without her.

To be honest, for all my prayers, I had never really found that connection with God and had not been conscious of His presence in my everyday life. I have always envied others who speak with a passion when it comes to their personal relationship with God. I wanted what they had, but I could never seem to have and feel that connection with Him.

One cold morning in January, I was walking around the park with my dog and started my day in the usual way, praying to God. I would ask Him for the normal things, like thanking him for another sober day and the strength and courage to handle any given situation or circumstance that I was having difficulty accepting. I asked Him to help me with my lack of patience and tolerance and other defects of character that needed some attention. My prayers were more repetitive each morning and evening. I would rattle them off without really thinking about what I was saying, like I was reading from a book. That morning, I spoke very differently to God, through sheer desperation I cried out to Him like I never had before.

I asked Him to reveal himself to me; I wanted to really get to know him, to feel his presence in my life. I begged Him to show me how to let go, how to get out of the driving seat and asked Him to take over. I explained how desperately I needed Him in my life and I was open to anything, I needed his love and guidance, my way had never worked. As uncomfortable as it was, I told Him that I doubted His existence, but only kept praying, just in case. I asked Him to show me how to let go. I handed my life and everything in it over to Him, without looking back. I begged Him to strengthen my trust.

I returned from the park and explained to my partner what had just happened. From that morning, my life has turned around in the most amazing way. In the beginning, I thought I was having a nervous breakdown, not realising that what I was experiencing was a spiritual awakening. It felt like some kind of transformation was taking place and it was out of my control. My self-awareness had become pretty intense, I thought I was going mad in the beginning, but have been reassured by others who have had similar experiences as mine, that this is normal. I pray on a different level these days, I sense that I am being heard. I have been more accepting of situations in my life and my loss of my dear mother is slowly becoming more manageable as time goes by. I still get overwhelmed with sadness when I allow myself to think of Mum, but I am learning to get a handle on my emotions, allowing the tears to come freely, for they are healing. I do not focus so much on the past these days and I take each day as it comes. Previously I was never able to stay focused on the day I was in, for fear of the future distracted me. My obsession for alcohol and drugs has left me but I will always watch out for complacency, for my demons are not that far away, they could return at anytime, like they have done in the past.

I have been with my partner for nearly four years now. Our relationship isn't perfect, but then who's is? Roger has his faults and I certainly have mine too. Many times, especially in the early days, I questioned whether he was right for me. Like I had done so many times in the past, I would focus on people's bad points, forgetting about the good qualities they had. Today I try to focus on the important things about that person and what they contribute to the relationship. I realise that I have to work at the relationship; it's about giving as well as taking. I am allowing someone else to love me; it feels so good just being me.

I view life very differently to how I did before. Since my mother passed away, I have realised how short life really is and that we are only here for a short while. I realise I have wasted so much of my life in and out of recovery and have hurt many people along the way. I have tried to make amends to as many people as I possibly can. For me, it is not so much about whether I will be forgiven, it is more important that I know, in my heart of hearts, that my behaviour when I was drinking alcohol was not the real me that I am getting to know. As long as I can forgive myself and strive to be the best that I can possibly be, that is good enough for me. The best gift I can give my amazing daughter is to remain clean and sober, one day at a time. I am hopeful for my future today, every day is a new beginning for me. I am discovering so much more about myself than I ever knew existed. I know that people can love me for who I really am. I don't need alcohol any more to give me that false sense of security. My security and wellbeing is my responsibility, nobody else's. It can't be bought or given to me. I owe it to myself to love and respect who I am and I deserve to be happy, just as we all do. I try not to take anything for granted today. The most important thing for me is my health – without this I can do nothing. Life is a gift, a gift so precious and I appreciate it more than anything else. I have been given many chances in my life but I threw them by the way side. As long as I do my best, God will take care of me, I have nothing to fear. What a revelation.

When I reflect back on my life, with all its ups and downs, I truly believe I have been tried and tested in so many different ways, but most importantly, I have survived it all. I am so blessed and feel privileged to have been given the opportunity to share my life story with you.

God bless you all.